Emily Dickinson

L. Dickinson

2763

Bonita E. Thayer

E·M·I·L·Y
DICKINSON

Franklin Watts
New York / London / Toronto / Sydney
An Impact Biography / 1989

Photographs courtesy of:
The Granger Collection: pp. 2, 24, 46, 81, 100;
Bettmann Archive: pp. 8 (both), 14, 35, 82, 92,
98, 104, 111; The Jones Library, Inc., Amherst:
pp. 12, 20, 56, 59, 76, 96, 113, 123; New York
Public Library Picture Collection: p. 108.

Library of Congress Cataloging-in-Publication Data

Thayer, Bonita E.
Emily Dickinson / Bonita E. Thayer.
p. cm.—(An Impact biography)
Bibliography: p.
Includes index.
Summary: Examines the life of the reclusive nineteenth-century
poet from Amherst, Massachusetts, whose posthumously published
poetry brought her the public attention she had carefully avoided
during her lifetime.
ISBN 0-531-10658-6
1. Dickinson, Emily, 1830–1886—Biography—Juvenile literature.
2. Poets, American—19th century—Biography—Juvenile literature.
[1. Dickinson, Emily, 1830–1886. 2. Poets, American.] I. Title.
PS1541.Z5T52   1989
811'.4—dc19   88-31376 CIP AC r88

Contents

Emily Dickinson

The young Emily
(left), Austin,
and Lavinia

Edward
Dickinson

Chapter

ONE

Emily Elizabeth Dickinson was born on December 10, 1830, in the little village of Amherst, Massachusetts. The village was in Hampshire county, 82 miles (131.2 km) from Boston. Her brother, William Austin Dickinson, was born April 16, 1829, and her sister, Lavinia Norcross Dickinson, was born on February 28, 1833.

Emily, Austin, and Vinnie were the ninth generation of Dickinsons in New England. In many ways, they were best friends as well as siblings. Emily and Austin had reddish-brown hair and brown eyes, like their father, while Vinnie was dark and pretty, like their mother.

Their father, Edward, was a respected lawyer. Sometimes the villagers called him "Squire" Dickinson, a sign of respect that pleased him. He was a stern head-of-the-house. He didn't smile much, and he expected his word to be obeyed without question. But there is little doubt that he loved his children very much. He showed his love in the way that they were reared and the things that he did for them.

Their mother, Emily Norcross Dickinson, was born in Monson, Massachusetts, the daughter of Joel and Betsy Fay Norcross. Betsy was described as pious, amiable, and useful. Her prudence, affection, and regard for the happiness of others were her most notable traits. A wife at the time was supposed to be modest, have an unassuming manner, and display a good disposition. She also had to know everything to do with domestic economy.

Edward Dickinson and Emily Norcross married on May 6, 1828, and set up housekeeping in the Widow Montague's home. It was a roomy and gracious environment for the young couple. Before long, they were expecting their first child.

Women then were not supposed to be seen in public when they were expecting a child. It was considered improper to expose oneself at any time during the pregnancy. A woman in that condition was thought to be unfit for polite, mixed society. Because of this, Emily could not go home to Monson when her oldest brother, Hiram, died of tuberculosis on February 26, 1829.

Tuberculosis was called consumption at that time, and the Norcross family lost a number of members to it. Emily's brothers, Eli (1809–1811) and Austin (1802–1824), died of it before her marriage.

Dr. Isaac Cutter came to the house to deliver William Austin Dickinson. After recovering from the birth, Emily took the infant and went home to Monson. Her mother had also contracted consumption. Emily was present when her mother died.

Back in Amherst, Emily discovered that the family would soon be moving. The mortgage on her father-in-law's home was getting too much for him to pay. By having the young couple move into it, the mansion might be saved. They moved in April 1830.

Being a housewife during this time was a full-time job. There was always more work than Emily had time to do. The peace and harmony of a household was built on the ceaseless toil of the women of the family.

Young Emily was born in the big yellow brick mansion on Main Street, built in 1813 by her grandfather, Samuel Fowler Dickinson. Noah Webster lived down the street from the mansion from 1812 to 1822, while he worked on his famous dictionary. He defined a mansion as a dwelling with four chimneys. The Dickinsons' dwelling had five. It also had a barn, a carriage shed, a large woodpile, and many trees and shrubs.

The family always called it the homestead. It was the first brick home built in Amherst, and young Emily loved it dearly. After Emily and Edward moved in, ownership was divided equally between Emily's father and grandfather. According to the deed on the mansion, the property line ran down the middle of the front hall and divided the mansion equally from garret to cellar.

Young Emily and Austin were able to move freely between the two halves and visit their grandmother, Lucretia Gunn Dickinson, whenever they wanted. They saw very little of their grandfather, but their proud grandmother often told them stories about the great deeds he had done. These stories were repeated later by their father, who

The Dickinson homestead in 1855

wanted them to remember the older man and what he stood for.

Samuel had graduated from Dartmouth College, second in the class of 1795 and the youngest graduate that year. He then returned to Amherst to practice law. He was a member of the state legislature, known in Massachusetts as the General Court, for several terms. He believed strongly in education for everyone, including women. This led to his being one of the founders of the Amherst Academy in 1814.

However, this was not enough for Samuel. He wanted all the citizens of Amherst to have access to higher education, and through his efforts, the cornerstone of the first building of Amherst College was laid on August 9, 1820. Noah Webster made the opening address.

Samuel was obsessed with the thought of the college. His law practice suffered because he was not available to run it. When money ran out and construction stopped, he furnished men and horses. He mortgaged his mansion to raise money for materials.

He only allowed himself four hours sleep a night. He would stay up studying and reading until midnight every night.

Classes began on September 19, 1821, even though the college was not chartered by the state of Massachusetts until February 21, 1825. By 1834, the college had 260 students. It was larger than Harvard and next in size to Yale.

There was widespread enthusiasm for the college. When Ralph Waldo Emerson visited it in 1823, he said in his journal, "The infant college is an infant Hercules. Never was so much striving,

Amherst College

outstretching and advancing in a literary cause as is exhibited here. . . ." He continued to write about the students, their spirit, and their achievements.

However, Samuel had neglected his practice too long and spent his money too freely. His continuing aid to the college finally cost him everything he had. In 1833, he could no longer make payments on the mansion and the mortgage was foreclosed on February 27, 1833.

The following day, Dr. Cutter came to the homestead and delivered Lavinia. Something went wrong during the delivery. There are no details, but mother and child were bedridden for several months. Since young Emily was only a little over the age of two, she was sent to Monson to stay with her mother's sister, Lavinia, until her mother was recovered enough to take care of her.

Uncle Hiram's widow, Amanda, was dying of consumption just as Hiram had. Aunt Lavinia was taking care of her, too, and Amanda's children, William and Emily Lavinia. It was women's work then to take care of the sick and dying. The doctors would come and look in on the patients, but often there was nothing they could do. There are reports that Amanda was bled often. This was a common treatment for many illnesses at the time.

By the time young Emily came home to Amherst in early June, her grandparents were gone. They had moved, with their youngest child Elizabeth, to Walnut Hills, Ohio. On May 22, the entire mansion was sold to David Mack, and his family moved into the half of the mansion Emily's family had lived in. Her own family moved into the half that her grandparents had lived in. Now they were tenants of the Macks.

This was all very confusing to Emily. She was a bright child, but she couldn't understand her mother's illness and the separation from her, then having to come back to a different home. She also could not understand why her grandparents were gone.

Emily never saw her grandparents again. Her grandfather died in Hudson, Ohio, on April 22, 1838, of the "bilious complaint," a term used to cover almost any disease of the liver. Her grandmother died in Enfield, Massachusetts, on May 11, 1840. Both bodies were moved at a later time to the cemetery just beyond the northern grounds of the mansion.

Emily was only three when the Macks moved into the mansion. It was difficult for her and Austin to understand why they didn't have free run of the house, as they'd had before, but they accepted it. Besides, they had their baby sister, Vinnie, to play with and tell stories to.

The children played around the grounds whenever they had time away from their chores. Emily loved plants of all kinds and knew the names of all the wildflowers in the grove. She and her best friend and neighbor, Abby Wood, had a playhouse there and spent many happy hours in and around it.

As they got older, there was not as much time for fun. The children all had chores assigned to them. One of Austin's jobs was to bring water from the well to the house. It had to be hand carried in buckets. He also had to bring in wood for the fireplaces and the cookstove. The family did all their cooking on that stove and also heated the water to wash the dishes after meals.

Austin had to keep a good supply of dry wood

on hand as well as some slightly green wood that was used to slow down a fast-burning fire. The firebox was on the side, with an ash pit under it. The ashes had to be removed from the ash pit regularly. They were used for many things, such as to make soap, to line pathways, to provide traction underfoot in the icy winters, and to plow into the garden in the summer to sweeten the soil.

There was a hot-water reservoir on the other side of the stove that provided a small but steady supply of hot water during the day for cleaning or washing. It was only enough hot water for a quick cleanup. Especially in the winter, this reservoir had to be kept full. As the water evaporated, it added moisture to the air and made it feel warmer.

When they wanted to bathe, extra water had to be brought in and heated on the stove. Then it was poured into a wooden tub that looked like a large round bucket, and the family took turns bathing in it.

Laundry days were the busiest of all, with never any time for play. There was more water to carry and more wood to be brought in to heat it. The clothes were scrubbed on a washboard. This was a wooden frame with a metal center that had ridges on it. The clothes were rubbed across these ridges until the stains were scrubbed out.

More water was needed for rinsing the clothes. Then they were wrung out by hand and hung outside on a line to dry. Underclothes were hung inside other clothing because it was not thought proper to hang underwear where anyone could see it.

In the winter, the clothes would freeze on the line. This also dried them. When brought into the house, they would thaw and be just damp enough to iron. The irons then were called sadirons. The "sad" part of the word meant compact and heavy, but the women joked that it meant it made them sad to iron. The irons were of the flatiron type, pointed at both ends. There were different weights and sizes for different jobs, and usually a removable handle that could be used for all of them. Some flatirons were very small and were used only for lace.

The irons were heated on the kitchen stove. When one of them was hot, it was used until it cooled off too much to remove any more wrinkles; then it was placed back on the stove to reheat while another one was used.

The girls had chores as soon as they were big enough to manage them. They set the table as soon as they could reach it. They helped wherever they could. Women and girls did all the housework. They had to bake bread, can fruits and vegetables in the summer, make jellies, and keep the house clean and ready for visitors who might appear at any time.

Emily and her family enjoyed having company, even though it meant extra work. Visitors arrived by stagecoach, like the mail did, or drove their own horses and buggies if they didn't live too far away. In the winter, every family had a sleigh that the horses could pull over the snow.

Emily loved the snow and winter games. She enjoyed coming in from the cold and being warmed by the fireplace. But her favorite time of year was spring, when all the flowers began to bloom and the whole world seemed to be coming to life after a long sleep. She always loved the spring—except for the one in 1840.

Chapter

❧TWO❧

Emily was nine years old in April 1840 when she learned that her family was going to move from the mansion. Her father and Deacon Mack had both decided that they needed more room for their families, so the Dickinsons moved.

The new house was only a short distance away, on North Pleasant Street. Emily was not leaving her friends nor the town she grew up in, but she felt that she was leaving a part of herself behind and she didn't want to move. She told Austin that it felt like her roots were being torn up. Austin tried to comfort her, but he, too, was sad about leaving the home that their grandfather had built and that they had lived in since they were born.

Even for such a short distance, the move was a lot of work. Their father hired two men to do the heavy work and a large wagon pulled by a team of horses. The family did all the packing.

Austin helped wrap the arms and legs of the mahogany furniture to protect them from

*The Dickinson house on
North Pleasant Street*

scratches. Emily had to go down in the hoarding cellar to wrap the jars of preserves, jellies, apple butter, and vegetables. There was also a barrel of apples, some potatoes, and some cabbages to be moved. She took a lantern filled with whale oil to light her way in the dark cellar and she took copies of the *Springfield Republican, Northampton Courier,* and *Hampshire Gazette* for wrapping the glass jars. She didn't take any copies of *Parley's Magazine* down with her. Her father had subscribed to it for the children, and they kept their copies to read over and over again.

Finally, the last load was on its way. All that was left was for the family to get into the buggy, hitched up to Edward's favorite mare, and drive to the new house. But Emily was nowhere to be found. Austin and his father went in search of her.

While they were looking, Edward confided to his son that his dream was to make enough money to pay off all of his father's debts and then one day buy back the mansion for the family. As the oldest of eight children, Edward felt that it was his duty. His father had been an idealist, but Edward was a realist. For now they had to leave, but someday they would move back. The move was a painful one for the adults, too.

They finally found Emily in the grove. She was staring hard at everything in hopes that she would never forget any part of it. They gently led her back to the waiting buggy. With her mother in a black silk dress and her father wearing his high beaver hat and a gold-headed cane by his side, they set off for the short trip to the wooden house on Pleasant Street.

Austin sympathized with Emily, but the new

house had something in it that made it very appealing to him—a pump in the kitchen. He couldn't help but be pleased that he no longer had to haul buckets of water. He still had to bring in wood for the kitchen stove and the fireplaces, but he didn't think that was nearly as bad as the water detail.

The children all kept busy in the garden hoeing the plants and watering them when needed. They also grew apples, peaches, pears, and grapes. There were chickens, too, that had to be tended to; they furnished the family with eggs for eating and baking.

That fall, Vinnie and Emily both left West Middle District Public School to attend the Amherst Academy, the three-story white-washed brick building their grandfather had founded. Every Wednesday they had to recite in front of an assembly. Emily was small, timid, and shy, but once she started reading, she lost herself in the words, and everyone enjoyed listening to her wonderful speaking voice.

Emily's mother often kept her out of school because she thought that Emily needed the rest and the fresh air. This was not uncommon at that time. There were no antibiotics and infectious diseases were not treatable. Every sore throat or bout of flu could mean death to the one afflicted.

Emily liked going to school. She studied Latin, mathematics, history, and geography along with mental and natural philosophy (the investigation of the truths and principles of being, knowledge, and conduct), ecclesiastical history (pertaining to the church and the clergy), and a variety of sciences. Botany was her favorite; she never felt she knew enough about her beloved plants.

There were four terms in the year. Each of

them was eleven weeks long, with two weeks off in between. Emily, in fun, signed her name as "Emilee" for a while during these carefree days.

Sometimes the children played at the home of Dr. Hitchcock, the president of the college. When they played "Blind-Man's Bluff," the taller boys would climb up onto a tall mantel in the kitchen to keep out of reach of the girls, including Dr. Hitchcock's daughter, Jane. Dr. Hitchcock was a naturalist, and Emily enjoyed hearing him talk about plant life almost as much as she liked to play games with the other children.

Every day at home, Emily's father led the family in prayer and read chapters from the Bible. They worshipped once or twice on Sunday at the yellow Congregational Church, where Emily's high-buttoned shoes would swing from the high, white-painted pews above the carpeted prayer cushions. Edward had purchased the pews in 1830, when the church was new.

There were two cast-iron box stoves to warm the church in the winter. There were also foot stoves to put embers in and rest one's feet on, and the women had muffs for their hands. Some people came from far away and couldn't go home between the morning and evening services on Sunday. They would eat lunch around the stoves and heat soapstones to put in their buggies or sleighs for warmth on the long ride home.

The church Emily attended was the Orthodox Trinitarian Congregational Church. The word "congregational," in this instance, referred to the kind of government the church had. Each congregation was responsible for itself and survived by its own merit. They were not connected to any other

Edward Hitchcock

church except in common religious beliefs. The members had to provide the funding and materials for the building of the church and its upkeep. They put out a call for a minister, hired one that they could agree on, and provided a place for him to live.

Emily thought the hymns were gloomy, made even more so by the bass viol that accompanied them. She had a certain terror of religion. The tolling of the church bells alarmed her, as did the sermons given by visiting ministers, who preached fire and brimstone. The minister's voice came from a pulpit so high up that it seemed to Emily to be coming from a spirit body floating above her head.

The sermons as well as the bedtime prayers encouraged a preoccupation with death. Preschoolers were taught to read from the *New England Primer*. There were prayers in this for them to learn. Some prayers talked of a burial place where there were smaller-than-average graves because young children die, too. These prayers warned that even children should be prepared for death.

Emily accepted some of the Puritan beliefs that were espoused at the time. She believed that God was everywhere and knew everything, and that He helped and inspired the human struggle for good over evil. However, while the preachers emphasized the evil in people, Emily looked around her and saw mostly the good.

She believed that you should do the best you can at whatever task you are working on, especially if it affects other people, even if you think it is a trivial task. She felt that all duties, even the most distasteful ones, should be treated equally in the way they were carried out.

Vinnie and Emily did the marketing for their mother. There were no paved streets, but there were gravel sidewalks to help them keep the mud from their shoes in wet weather. In dry weather, there was a coating of gray dust on everything, stirred up by carriage wheels.

From their house they walked past white picket fences that were around almost every yard, and the great marshy common used for pasturing cows and other grazing animals. They looked in the window of Mr. Pierce's shoe store, where ladies' lasting gaiters, which were coverings of cloth or leather for the foot and sometimes the lower leg, and velvet shoes were sold. Their main destination was Cutler's Dry Goods store, which sold everything from bonnet silk to paint and groceries.

They had a list from their mother and only had to tell the clerk what they wanted. The clerk wrapped up their purchases and wrote down their cost on a sheet he kept. Later he would send Edward a bill listing all the items purchased. Women were not expected to pay bills or handle large sums of money. Usually, the woman of the house was provided with $1 a week "pin" money. Any change that they received into their gloved hands was washed before it was spent.

In the very center of town, under the swinging wooden sign of the Boltwood Tavern, were the stopping places for the horses and carriages of two stagecoach lines. One line ran north and south from Brattleboro to Hartford; the other ran east and west from Boston to Albany.

The stagecoach drivers had a kind of romance about them. They lived and worked under great pressure, driving the four black horses 20 miles (32 km) every day. The regular stagecoach had three seats inside, with cushions and room for three passengers on each. There was room for one more outside with the driver, for a total of ten passengers.

The mail coach required the greatest speed. It held three passengers in a special compartment on springs at the front of the coach behind the driver. This was sometimes called the "monkey box." The mailbags were carried in a long wooden box resting without springs on the wheels' axles. These were not in use very long, as the regular coaches were more practical.

The drivers were well dressed, in hats and tailored clothing made of expensive fabric. Their boots and belts were made from good leather and usually finely tooled. No one could work for the stagecoach lines unless he had a reputation for honesty and dependability. The drivers drank 5¢ glasses of whiskey instead of the regular 3¢ ones the others drank. Since they brought the mail, and often guests, the girls liked to be there when the stages came in. They would then run home and tell their mother who in the town was having company.

Edward became involved in politics, believing that it was a way to help his town as well as his country. In 1840, he campaigned for presidential candidate William Henry Harrison, a Whig. In the fall of 1841, he went to the Whig convention at North Umpton, the county seat, and was nominated for the state senate. His running mate was Samuel Williston from Easthampton, the man who had started the seminary there.

Edward won the election, and beginning in 1842, he and Williston had to go to Boston for weeks at a time. When the legislature adjourned in March, they came home.

Emily missed having her father at home. Austin was left as the man of the family while their father was away. In April, soon after Edward returned home, Austin was taken out of the academy and sent to spend the spring term at Williston's seminary. This was the first time the children had been apart, and Emily especially missed her brother. She wrote him many letters.

Austin came home when the term ended in August, and the family was happy to be together again. When the legislature reconvened in September, Edward had to return to Boston. Since he was to be gone again, he decided that Austin should stay at home with the women and go to the academy rather than returning to the seminary. His decision pleased everyone.

Chapter

✤THREE✤

The Dickinson orchard adjoined a burial ground. Every funeral procession passed their house. Smallpox, cholera, scarlet fever, and typhoid fever took many young lives. These diseases were considered to be sent from God as punishment for sins. People used fasting, humiliation, and prayer to combat what they considered almost inevitable.

Each house had its privy—sometimes called an outhouse—a small wooden structure used for a toilet. There were anywhere from one to three seats inside with holes cut in them. When there was more than one seat, the holes were usually of various diameters so that even the youngest members of the family could sit in comfort. Each house also had its own well. No one realized that the holes dug under the privies and the holes dug for the wells were often on the same level underground, and that waste from the privy could contaminate the drinking water. This contamination was a major cause of cholera.

It was thought that a woolen bandage worn around and below the waist, encircling the abdomen, was of great value in warding off all kinds of sickness in summer. Many people died young. Most of the remedies used to cure illness were often worse than the disease itself. For cholera, equal parts of tincture of opium (called laudanum then), rhubarb, capsicum (obtained from hot peppers and still used today in some stomach remedies), camphor, spirits of nitre (nitrate of potash), and essence of peppermint—double strength—were mixed. The dosage was five to thirty drops every fifteen minutes.

To cure a cough, sore throat, sore chest, or kidney difficulties a recipe called "Peckham's Balsam" was used. It included 3 pounds (1.36 kg) of clear, pale rosin; 1 quart spirits of turpentine; 1 ounce balsam of tolu (a fragrant resin from a South American tree, used as an expectorant); 4 ounces balsam of fir (a sap from the North American fir tree); 1 ounce each of oil of hemlock (a poisonous herb used in small amounts as a powerful sedative), origanum (a wild herb), and Venice turpentine; and 4 ounces of strained honey. The dose was six to twelve drops at a time and could be varied according to the ability of the stomach to bear it and the severity of the case.

Just after Emily's thirteenth birthday, two of her mother's friends died a month apart. Then, a month later, Emily's friend, Sophia Holland, became ill with "brain fever." Emily sat vigil, called a "watch," by her fifteen-year-old friend's bedside.

This was not unusual. In fact, it was considered standard preparation and training for womanhood in the nineteenth century. Emily was made to leave when the dying child's "reason fled." Emily, deeply affected by the death of her friend, began searching for answers to why it had happened. She slipped into a deep depression and her parents sent her to her Aunt Lavinia in Boston to try to revive her spirits. It was very difficult for Emily to come to terms with the death of her friend, especially when the religion she was being taught spoke of a person's guilt and how a person must be repentant and beg to be spared the punishment he or she deserved after death. Emily could not believe that Sophia deserved punishment for anything.

On her return from Boston, Emily was given a big square rosewood piano with three pedals and a matching stool. She loved the piano and practiced two hours every day, even on school days. She would usually play joyous, light music rather than the solemn music she always heard at church. Her father, pleased with her dedication, would read the paper in the evening while she played.

Emily had a close friend, Helen Fiske, who was opposite in almost every way from her. Helen was robust and healthy, loved to wander off on twisting roads, and found strange people fascinating. Emily worried about her friend's health, even though Emily herself was the frailer of the two. The Fiskes lived within walking distance of the Dickinsons, and the girls saw each other often until the Fiske family moved when the girls were eleven.

When Helen was thirteen, her mother died. Four years later, her father died, and she went to live with an aunt in Falmouth. The girls lost touch with each other for a while.

In 1844, Lyman Coleman came to Amherst to take charge of the Amherst Academy. He was married to Maria Flynt of Monson, a cousin of Emily's mother. Their two daughters—Olivia, seventeen, and Eliza, twelve—became friends with Emily and Vinnie. When they moved to Amherst, both Coleman girls had consumption and were watched closely by their parents.

When Emily turned fifteen in 1845, she pinned up her hair and put it under a net cap. She had to start dressing and acting like an adult. No lady ever wore more than seven colors at one time. Seven colors were enough for a rainbow, and no one should ever try to outdo God. The girls were also not supposed to wear clouded stockings with a white dress, or pink bonnets. The hem of a gown had to cover the ankles.

Emily finally learned to tell time by the clock. Her father thought that he had taught her, but she had not understood him. She was afraid to tell him and afraid to tell anyone else for fear that they would tell him and he would be angry.

She and Vinnie were helping with all the housework now. Domestic activity, as mentioned earlier, was a full-time job, and all the duties had to be performed in skirts that swept the floor and often measured 10 yards (9 m) around the bottom.

Emily could no longer run and play as she had, since that was considered unseemly for a young lady. She also had to wear a bonnet or carry a parasol whenever she went outside, as ladies were not supposed to have tans.

Amherst had a reputation for literacy at a time when over half the adult population of the United States could neither read nor write in any language. There were approximately 400 families living in

Amherst. Over 600 people had newspaper subscriptions, 265 subscribed to periodicals, and 550 to religious publications. There were 515 registered voters. Amherst did not even have a bank until 1864, but it did have the J. S. & C. Adams of Amherst bookstore. This was the gathering place of the learned in the village.

This atmosphere that encouraged education was due in large part to Emily's family. Her grandfather and her father both believed in education and independent thought, for women as well as for men. Edward had entered Amherst College as a sophomore the year it opened, and he transferred to Yale shortly thereafter, graduating in 1823 as valedictorian. Joel Norcross, Emily's maternal grandfather, was a leader and benefactor of the town of Monson, Massachusetts, and was a founder of the Monson Academy.

Edward did not believe in light reading, but Emily's curiosity was stronger than her fear of disappointing him. Mr. Humphry, a teacher, lent her several books of this type from his library; she hid them in her room.

There was a winter religious revival, and Emily was deeply affected by it but did not "convert." For converting, a person was supposed to humble himself or herself and plead to be spared the punishment that he or she deserved for real or imagined sins. When the person was certain of forgiveness, he or she was considered worthy to join the church.

In refusing to convert, Emily had started her rebellion against certain Puritan beliefs, a rebellion that would last the rest of her life. Prayer gave her strength, but she had been made to fear her own "wicked ways." Because she was so well read and encouraged to learn, however, she could not help but question all that was going on around her.

She visited her aunt in Boston for four weeks and went sightseeing, attended two concerts and a horticultural exhibit, and also visited the Chinese museum there. In the museum were a number of life-size wax figures representing all classes of Chinese people, a collection of Chinese paintings and home furnishings, and models of pagodas, temples, and bridges.

With her background and family, it is no surprise that Emily decided to attend Mount Holyoke Seminary in South Hadley, a boarding school favored by her father, who believed that every girl should have the experience of a good school away from home. Emily studied very hard so that she could pass the three days of entrance exams required for admission. She did not want to disappoint her family by not passing, nor did she want to lose a chance for an exciting new adventure in her life.

The fall before her seventeenth birthday in 1847, her father drove her in the buggy to Mount Holyoke. The 10-mile (16-km) drive took one and one-half hours in good weather. She passed the difficult tests and was admitted as a student.

The school was in a four-story brick building with a two-story portico in front. It had first opened its doors in 1837. Its founder and principal was Mary Mason Lyon, an evangelist who tried to convert all the girls and train the young women to be missionaries.

Emily shared a room with her cousin, Emily Norcross. This was the same cousin Emily had

Mount Holyoke Seminary

played with in Monson when her mother was sick after the birth of Vinnie. Emily Norcross's mother had died by now, but Grandfather Norcross made sure that the orphan grandchildren received an education.

The two cousins and the other 298 pupils did all the domestic work at the school. Emily's assigned duty was to gather up the knives from the first tier of tables after breakfast and dinner and wash and polish them.

The girls had a very rigid schedule. Everyone rose at 6 A.M. and ate breakfast at 7. Study period was from 8 to 9, after which they went to the devotions held in Seminary Hall. They reviewed ancient history at 10:15 and at noon had calisthenics for the half-hour before dinner. They all studied until supper at 6 P.M., and they were all in bed by 9.

In spite of being surrounded by people, her days filled with new things to learn, Emily got very homesick. She had never been away from her home and family before. She and her cousin, Emily, got along very well, but it was not the same. Her family and friends missed her, too. Two weeks after she started classes, Austin, Vinnie, and Abby Wood came to visit her. They brought goodies from home—cakes and fruits—but mostly they brought themselves, as medicine to relieve the homesickness Emily was feeling.

Life was so different and structured at the school. Emily missed the newspapers she was used to reading daily. She missed the discussions of politics and world affairs that her family had at the supper table. She felt at times that she and the entire school were cut off from the rest of the world. On October 21, 1847, she half-jokingly wrote to Austin:

Won't you please to tell me when you answer my letter who the candidate for President is? I have been trying to find out ever since I came here & have not yet succeeded. I dont know anything more about affairs in the world, than if I was in a trance, & you must imagine with all your 'Sophomoric discernment,' that it is but little & very faint. Has the Mexican war terminated yet & how? Are we beat? Do you know of any nation about to besiege South Hadley? If so, inform me of it, for I would be glad of a chance to escape, if we are to be stormed. I suppose Miss Lyon would furnish us all with daggers & order us to fight for our lives, in case such perils should befall us.[1]

In November, her mother and father paid her a surprise visit. She spotted them from her window as they got out of their carriage. She danced, clapped her hands with joy, and flew to meet them.

She did go home for Thanksgiving and was very happy to be there. It was a big family celebration. When she returned to school to begin her second term, she started English composition. Her papers were often marked "original." Some of her originality and independence would cause her difficulties later in life.

[1] Polly Longsworth, *Emily Dickinson: Her Letters to the World*, (New York: Thomas Y. Crowell Company, 1965).

Christmas was considered a pagan holiday by the Congregationalists. The school declared that students were to spend the day in their rooms, fasting and meditating. Emily rebelled at this. If the day was considered a pagan holiday, then why should it be given any notice at all? It would be better to ignore it and carry on like any other day. She took the afternoon stage to Amherst.

When she returned to school, she found that a public declaration of faith was expected. Without it, the girls could not be considered members of the church but only unsaved sinners. All the girls who wanted to "become Christians" and be converted to the faith were asked to stand. Emily alone remained seated. It was not that she didn't want to become a Christian; she just could not make the declaration that was expected. Since she could not accept all the tenets of the Congregationalist faith, she did not feel that she could honestly stand up and be counted. It depressed her and made her feel she was a "bad" person because she could not feel and react the way others said a person should. The sermons about death and judgment scared her, but she knew in her heart that lying would do nothing for her soul.

Chapter

❖FOUR❖

In January 1848, Emily underwent another religious crisis but remained unconverted. The other girls tried to be understanding, but it didn't help.

One of the rules of the seminary was that the young ladies could not make or receive calls on Sunday, the Sabbath, as that was the day that God had finished his work and rested. God then blessed the seventh day and hallowed it, and it was to be used as a day of rest and worship. Nor could they spend a single Sabbath away from the seminary during the term. The reason given for this was that the place of weekly labors was the best spot to appreciate and understand the meaning of the Sabbath. If the girls went home (or anywhere else), they might not give the proper respect to the day but enjoy themselves instead. Emily resented not being able to go home on the weekends and spend the Sabbath with her family. She did not like other people declaring what was right for her.

Many people believed at the time that a woman was not supposed to have a mind of her own.

Recreation was not meant for womenfolk. Their business was to attend to the household work, to fear the Lord, and to hold their tongues.

Valentines were forbidden at school. The girls were not supposed to get or give them. Many of them walked to the post office anyway and mailed the illegal missives. The ones they received were shared later in their rooms, the thrill of breaking a rule almost as great as the valentines themselves. Valentines were not purchased then. They were handwritten and personal. The girls would sometimes decorate the valentines with little drawings or pressed flowers.

In March, Emily developed a racking cough. She couldn't seem to shake whatever was causing it. She didn't complain or mention it in her letters home. However, a visitor to one of the other girls noticed it and reported her condition to her father. Edward immediately sent Austin to bring Emily home, over her protests. Austin probably went after her in the family cabriolet, a light, two-wheeled, one-horse carriage capable of seating two people. It was lined with cream-colored broadcloth with high doors and oval windows at the sides and back.

During the month that it took for Emily to get well, her father gave her daily doses of medicine. She commented to a friend on how vile the medication was. The recipe for cough syrup was 1 ounce essence of hemlock, 2 ounces of castor oil, and 1 teaspoon of camphor, mixed thoroughly and added to 1 pint of molasses. The patient was given one teaspoon four to six times a day. After the cough was gone, Edward made Emily stay home another month to build up her strength.

While Emily had been away at school, Benjamin

Newton had come to study law with her father. She became acquainted with him while she was home sick. He admired her quick mind and her love of words. He recommended that she read Moore's *The Epicurean*, Longfellow's *Evangeline*, and other books. She kept up with her studies while she was home, and when she returned to school in May, she was not behind in anything. She finished the term in August. She loved the school, her studies, her teachers, and the other young women, but she was nevertheless relieved when her father decided not to send her for another term. She missed her family too much when she was away, and the fact that she alone had not converted made her feel apart from her classmates.

After her education was completed, a woman was expected to live at home with her parents until she married. This was fine with Emily. That fall she spent a lot of time alone in her room. She needed time to think and to sort out her feelings. Newton had enlarged her thoughts, but she had to keep most of her new ideas to herself, as her father would not understand why she would believe anything other than what she had been taught to believe. Newton realized this and hid books for her in the bushes by the front door.

Newton was something of an advanced thinker and very much a reader of contemporary literature. As his friendship with Emily developed, he pushed her to expand her thoughts into worlds from which she'd been sheltered. For example, he gave her Lydia Maria Child's socially radical book, *Letters From New York*.

From that book, and later from Ralph Waldo Emerson's writings and poems, she found the liberating notions of self-reliance, personal experience over tradition, and the concept of poet as "seer," or prophet.

Newton stirred her poetic leanings and gave her the support and encouragement she needed to lead the life she chose. He encouraged her to stretch spiritually and intellectually beyond her limited experiences.

Vinnie and Austin also read the books Newton gave Emily. Then Austin brought home a copy of Longfellow's romance *Kavanagh*, borrowed from a fraternity brother. The story of a young minister and two girls who fell in love with him, the book tended to satirize life in the small towns of New England.

Austin passed the book to Emily, but Edward saw him and intercepted it. When he saw what it was, he did not forbid them to read it but did tell them he thought it was unsuitable and requested that they return it unread. They could feel his disapproval, but they read it anyway. They read many more books after that that would not have met with his approval, either. Emily adored her father, but she would not close her mind for him. It was Edward himself who had wanted his children independent, their minds free. It was he who made them think for themselves even if it meant disagreeing with him.

Whenever Edward wanted to show his children his displeasure with them, he would take his hat and cane and leave the house in silence. It was a wordless censure but very effective. The children never had any doubt as to his feelings when he left.

In 1848 two books were published by authors that Emily admired and that had an influence on her—*Wuthering Heights* by Emily Brontë and *Jane Eyre* by Charlotte Brontë. Emily delighted in the stories themselves but also liked the way the women used words to convey their thoughts. Emily thought it was wonderful that the Brontë sisters were getting the recognition they deserved. Their books were very popular. *Wuthering Heights* was the last book Emily Brontë wrote. She died in December of that year from consumption.

By 1849, Emily and Newton were spending a lot of time together. They shared his books and their views on authors and ideas. Emily knew that, in general, if a woman wanted to win a husband, she was expected to "put her brains up under a net cap," along with her hair. However, she knew that Newton was different. He expected Emily to be herself and to use all the intelligence she had.

They didn't spend all their time reading books. In March, they went to the "sugaring off." No one had planted the maple trees. They grew wild, and Emily felt that the annual harvest from them was even sweeter because it was a gift from the trees she loved.

It took at least forty years for a maple tree to reach 10 inches (25 cm) in diameter, the minimum needed at the butt to tap it. Larger trees could be two or even three hundred years old. Some of the older trees that were cut down showed the tomahawk cuts where the Indians had tapped the trees before white people came. The Indians cut slashes in the trees, collected the sap, and boiled it down in a hollowed-out cooking log above heated rocks. A good maple tree yielded 15 to 20 gallons (57 to 76 l) of sap in a sugaring season. That was enough to make about 2 quarts of pure maple syrup.

Great iron kettles were used to boil the sap.

Everyone stayed close to the fire for warmth and the delicious odor. Boiling down the sap was a lot of work. It took about one-quarter of a cord of wood burned for every 4 gallons (15 l) of syrup produced. The water in the sap evaporated and the syrup remained. If it was left to boil longer and get hotter, soft maple sugar formed. Longer and hotter yet, and hard maple sugar formed. What Emily and her friends were after was a confection called Jack Wax. The hot syrup was poured onto snow or ice, turning it into a taffy-like candy all of them loved.

Emily's father felt that there was too much contact between Emily and Newton. Perhaps he thought that without Newton's influence, Emily might settle more easily into her expected role. Or, he might have been afraid that she would marry Newton and he would lose her affection.

For whatever reason, he put in a recommendation for Newton to study with a retired judge from Worcester, the town Newton was from. Newton felt he had no choice but to accept the position and left in August. Before he went he told Austin he believed Emily had a wonderful, if rather strange, mind. She used words like no one he had ever known before and with perfect economy.

Emily had shown Newton pieces that she had written in school. He was impressed and had told her that she had the power to be a poet. She missed him terribly when he was gone.

Emily liked to study *Webster's Unabridged Dictionary* (the enlarged edition of 1847). She called it her Lexicon and took it with her everywhere. She would pore over it, delighting in finding new words. She read it the way others read novels.

Noah Webster was a lexicographer. He did not create words but captured them as they flew by in conversation. He labored for twenty years, at his own expense, to create the complete two-volume edition published in 1828. It was a handwritten manuscript with 70,000 listings.

He studied and mastered twenty-six languages, which helped him unearth the origins of many English words. The two-volume set sold for $20. This was a lot of money then and out of reach for most people. His heirs sold the rights to G. & C. Merriam Publishers, and they added illustrations. They also lowered the price to $6, making the books available to many more people. The emperor of Japan even ordered five hundred copies.

Since Webster had lived in Amherst from 1812 to 1822 and had been so active in village affairs and the town's educational system, he was looked upon as a local celebrity. To Emily, he was even more. He was the man who gave her many of the words she would use the rest of her life—words she could play with, experiment with, and enjoy for many years.

Lavinia turned sixteen in 1849, and the week after Thanksgiving she entered the Ipswich Female Seminary in Ipswich, Massachusetts, 125 miles (201 km) away. She just missed seeing Emily's old friend Helen Fiske, who left the school a short time before Vinnie arrived.

Vinnie roomed with Jane Hitchcock, daughter of President Hitchcock of Amherst College, at the house of Mrs. Ephraim Kendall. Families who had girls living with them did not take in other boarders. The charge for Vinnie's room and board was $1.25 a week. Every student was required to have an

English dictionary, a modern atlas, the Bible, one table- or dessertspoon, and one teaspoon.

At the seminary, the girls were taught self-control. They were told they were not placed in this world to have a good time but to do the Lord's work and to earn their way to heaven. Their daily devotions would help them.

With Vinnie away from home, Emily grew very lonely. To help this, her father bought her a Newfoundland dog. Carlo, as she named him, became her constant companion. Emily would smile to herself, thinking of the reaction Vinnie would have when she returned home. Vinnie had always favored cats and had them around her ankles most of the time.

Newton sent Emily a copy of Ralph Waldo Emerson's *Poems*. Emerson was at the height of his career when the book was published in 1847.

Emily sent a humorous letter in the form of a prose valentine to George Gould at the *Indicator*, the Amherst College monthly. He was on the editorial board, and she had had many animated talks with him. The valentine was printed anonymously, but she used Carlo's name in it so that her brother Austin would know who had written it. Austin was the one person she felt she could always count on to understand and appreciate her mind and her wit.

Noah Webster

Chapter

✤FIVE✤

In 1850 there was a great religious revival in New England. No person was considered a Christian simply by birthright. It was a condition that could only be arrived at by constant striving and, finally, some inner personal knowledge of God's grace and an awareness of His presence in the person's life.

Conversion was broken down into four steps. The first step was to feel guilt. People were to search deep within themselves and dredge up all the sins they could find. Next, they were to go through a period of despair and struggle as they realized how sinful they really were. The third step was the surrendering of their will to the Lord. If they had done everything correctly, the fourth step would come automatically, a sudden benediction of peace as sinners threw themselves on God's mercy and accepted Christ as the redeemer. They would be willing to accept the guiding hand of the Holy Spirit and know without a doubt that they had been forgiven their sins.

The revival meetings went on and on, and Emily's father attended more and more often. When he was forty-seven, he accepted Christ and joined the First Church of Christ. Mrs. Dickinson had joined in 1831, three years after her marriage. Emily thought a lot about it, read a lot about it, and asked penetrating questions. However, she was more interested in learning about religion than in being converted. It didn't matter to her who, or how many, converted; she couldn't do so until she could settle matters within herself.

Emily called herself "one of the lingering bad ones," because she did not follow the dictates of her society. According to most of the people around her, a person was good or bad, saved or not. Emily continued to go to church, but she had her own idea of God and her own way of worshipping. She was bothered by her lack of guilt. She saw many innocent people searching for this same guilt in themselves, searching until they were convinced of their own impurity.

Emily believed in God. She believed that He was with her and knew of her inner struggle. While others attended the revivals and loudly proclaimed their sins, Emily recalled the psalm that said, "Be still and know that I am God." She had to have had tremendous inner strength to remain unswayed by all that was happening around her.

Vinnie came home in mid-March for a visit. She and Austin were fascinated by the revival meetings. These meetings were basically founded to uphold the Puritan faith after Harvard became "infected" with Unitarianism. Emily's parents went to the meetings and Vinnie joined the church while she was home.

Emily held herself aloof, preferring the solitude of home and her books. This did not mean that she wasn't thinking about God. In a note to a friend, she wrote that her folks had all gone away, and they had been afraid that she would be lonely. But she wasn't, because God was there with her looking into her very soul to see if she thought right thoughts. She was not afraid because she tried to be upright and good and He knew every one of her struggles.

Her letters were not all solemn, though. She loved having fun with words. She wrote to another friend about garden snakes. "I love the little green ones that slide around by your shoes in the grass, and make it rustle with their elbows." Of course, snakes don't really have elbows, but Emily could almost make us believe that they did.

At this time the citizens of the town became especially concerned with protecting youths against themselves. All the taverns in town were closed, so that young men coming there to college would not have their lives ruined by drink. The Maine Law, passed in 1851—the first law prohibiting the sale of intoxicating liquors—was cheered by the citizens of Amherst, who believed in temperance, the total avoidance of intoxicating liquor as a beverage. When the town toasted Daniel Webster at the 1851 cattle show as "the friend of labor, champion of free Republican Institutions, and a friend of man," the toast was made with water.

The few citizens who felt the need for alcohol went to the druggist and had him mix his own special cough remedy. It was mostly alcohol with a little coloring and flavoring added. When the sale of liquor as a beverage was banned, cough remedy sales increased considerably.

The citizens didn't have to concern themselves with saving the women of the town from liquor. Ladies did not frequent taverns nor drink strong liquor. There was a certain amount of wine-making that went on in various homes, including the Dickinsons', but everyone managed to overlook this fact.

Vinnie returned to school in Ipswich. Their mother became ill with acute neuralgia, a nerve disease. With Vinnie gone, the burden of caring for her fell to Emily alone. Emily also had the other duties of the household to perform. She loved making bread. Her father would not eat bread baked by anyone other than Emily.

The wood stove had a warming oven where the bread was put to rise. It was about at eye level near the stovepipe. This warming oven was used to keep food warm. The heat of the oven itself was tested in a couple of different ways. If Emily could hold her hand in it for forty-five to sixty seconds, the oven was not very warm. If she had to remove her hand in thirty-five to forty-five seconds, it was moderately warm. If she could only stand it for twenty to twenty-five seconds, the oven was hot.

The other test was to put a piece of white paper in the oven for five minutes. If it turned pale yellow, it was just the right temperature for sponge cake; dark yellow was right for bread, and brown was perfect for cookies. The dry radiant heat of the wood stove was especially good for baking bread.

Emily always said that "Home is a holy thing."

She considered it her life's work "to make things pleasant for Father and Austin." The men were not to be disturbed with the everyday problems of running a home. In fact, if they were seen coming up the walk, the women would scurry to remove all traces of any cleaning implements. The home was a haven for the men.

Emily did not like housework. She would write of "scaring the timorous dust." She had to make her own cleaning supplies. A mixture of wax and turpentine was used for polishing the furniture. Homemade soap was used for washing floors, woodwork, and everything else that they thought needed cleaning. After the dishes were done, the water was dumped out the back door to water the flowers there or to clean the steps.

Now, with Vinnie away, Emily was caring for her mother and cooking for Austin and her father as best she could, but that didn't mean that she liked it. In another note she wrote, "*My* kitchen, I think I called it—God forbid that it was, or shall be my own—God keep me from what they call *households*, except that bright one of 'faith.' "

There were no "fast foods" in those days, and each meal was a rather elaborate affair that took an enormous amount of time to prepare. A typical main meal consisted of a soup course, followed by meat with gravy (fish on Friday), chicken, jellies, jams, cranberry sauce with meat pudding, and pie for dessert. Coffee was served throughout the meal. There were a number of vegetables served as side dishes that had to be prepared fresh from the garden or taken from jars in the cellar that the women had filled in the growing season.

Everything was done with a stove that had no thermostat nor any heat controls on the burners. There were a series of dampers and draft regulators to permit heat adjustments. There were lids for all the burners. There was one lid lifter. To fry something quickly, one of the burner lids would be lifted and the skillet would be put directly over the firebox flames. For slow cooking, the lid was left on and a cooler burner farther away from the firebox was used. A stock pot was left simmering on one of the back burners. All the leftovers went into it, and it was ready to eat at anytime. It changed daily as new things were added. Potatoes could be baked by burying them in the ashes under the hot fire in the firebox.

The fire had to be banked and the stovepipe damper closed to hold the fire overnight. That way, it only took a little time to get the stove hot and ready to cook breakfast the next day.

Since cooking took so much time and work, it is no wonder that Emily didn't like to do it. She still had the rest of the house to take care of and very little time for herself.

That year, Emily became friends with Susan Huntington Gilbert. Susan was only nine days younger than Emily, but her life had been very different. When Susan was two years old, her mother, Harriet Arms Gilbert, and her father, Thomas Gilbert, had moved to Amherst. Her father was a tavern keeper and came to be the proprietor of the Mansion House, a livery stable and tavern on Main Street. That same year, Sue's seven-year-old sister, Sophia, died. Four years later, Sue's mother died of consumption at the age of forty-five. The family broke up, and Sue was sent to be reared by her Aunt Sophia and Uncle William Van Vranken in Geneva, New York.

Five years later, Sue's father died and was listed as an insolvent debtor. Sue was ashamed and had very low self-esteem when at sixteen she returned to Amherst to live with a married sister and go to school. She felt that her father's life and the debts he left behind when he died reflected on her. Sue was also attending the revival meetings and had joined the church at the same time Emily's father did.

Emily had been writing poems for some time, usually for herself but occasionally for a friend, in a letter. When Sue's sister, Mary, died in July of 1850, Emily wrote a letter to Sue to console her and concluded the letter with her first solemn poem, which begins, "I have a Bird in spring/ Which for myself doth sing." The poem ends, "Then will I not repine,/ Knowing that Bird of mine/ Though flown/ Shall in a distant tree/ Bright melody for me/ Return."

Austin graduated from Amherst College in 1850. It was a cause for great celebration. Austin would miss the college days and Dr. Hitchcock, who was an ordained minister and also a professor of chemistry and natural history who drew his students' attention to the many wonders of the world around them and showed them how the study of nature could uplift the spirits.

Dr. Hitchcock also gave public lectures on hilltops. Many people attended. When he suggested that shade trees would improve the appearance of Amherst, it wasn't very long before 430 trees, mostly white pine, were transplanted from the forest to the village and the college grounds. It is no wonder that he had an influence on Austin as well as on Emily. When Austin later had his own home, he planted a grove of white pines on the property.

During receptions at the Hitchcocks, Emily Fowler, granddaughter of Noah Webster, sang for the entertainment of all. Vinnie liked to sing, too. She would sing at the parties held by the Sweetsers. Sweetser's parlor set the standards for elegance, as did Mrs. Sweetser, who would "receive" in purple gloves and make a long, dipping, backwards curtsy to each guest, a gesture she had learned at boarding school.

After he graduated, Austin took a teaching job in Sunderland, a village 10 miles (16 km) north of Amherst, for a year. Emily wrote to him often. She told him a lot about her new friend, Susan Gilbert. Austin became anxious to meet Sue, and when he did, he found that he liked her as well as Emily did. When he went to Boston to teach school (in 1851 and 1852), he wrote to Sue as often as he did to his family. Emily often called Sue "sister" because of the deep friendship that had developed between them. She encouraged the relationship between Austin and Sue.

During the summer of 1851, Jenny Lind, called the Swedish Nightingale by the newspapers, performed at the First Congregational Church in Northampton. Emily, Vinnie, and their parents traveled by stage for more than an hour over dirt roads to hear her. Emily was enthralled. Jenny's voice was like that of a child's, sweet and touching. She had been brought to the United States by Phineas T. Barnum, a master showman and pro-

moter. Over 30,000 people surrounded Lind's New York City hotel, trying to get a glimpse of the coloratura soprano. Tickets for her New York debut on September 11, 1850, at the Castle Garden theater were auctioned at $225 apiece. When tickets were auctioned in Boston, the top bid was $625. She gave ninety-five concerts around the country from 1850 to 1852, for which she received $17,675. Barnum made a fortune.

In September, Emily and Vinnie visited their aunt and cousins in Boston. They were glad to see them and also to be able to visit with their beloved brother, Austin. After this visit, Austin wrote to Sue and told her that Emily seemed to believe that the world outside of Amherst was hollow and, in many ways, fearful.

Emily sent a mock valentine, a poem, to William Howland, who was practicing law in Springfield. He had earlier studied law in Edward's office. He gave the poem to Dr. Josiah Gilbert Holland, the literary editor of the *Springfield Republican*. Dr. Holland published the poem, "Sic Transit," on February 20, 1852, with the full thirteen stanzas on the editorial page. He prefaced it with, "The hand that wrote the following amusing medley to a gentleman friend of ours as a valentine, is capable of writing very fine things and there is certainly no presumption in entertaining a private wish that a correspondence more direct than this be established between it and the *Republican*."

Austin Dickinson

Emily's name was not given in the paper, but Amherst readers knew the poem was hers. She chose not to become a contributor to the paper, however, though later she became friends with Dr. Holland and his wife, Elizabeth.

Dr. Holland had studied medicine and, after the prescribed two years of training, began his practice in Springfield. He married Elizabeth Chapin in 1845. Both he and Elizabeth were outgoing and had many friends.

Soon he realized that his hobby of writing poems and prose sketches was absorbing more and more of his time and interest. He eventually abandoned his medical practice and took a trip through the South. He sent back lively accounts of his travels, which were published in installments in the *Springfield Daily Republican.*

When he returned to Springfield in 1849, at editor Sam Bowles' invitation, he became the associate editor of the newspaper. By the time he was thirty, he was established in his career. Amherst College conferred an honorary Master of Arts degree on him. He was nationally known as an author and a lecturer by the time he was forty.

Austin had taken a teaching position in Boston in 1851. He was still unsure of the direction his life would take. There were many letters back and forth between him and his family and, of course, Sue.

In 1851, Emily wrote to Austin that Hepzibah and Clifford in Nathaniel Hawthorne's *House of the*

Josiah Holland

[58]

Seven Gables made her recall their own relationship. She always felt that the Dickinsons were different, especially she and Austin. They were both attracted to the arts—she in her writing, he in his collecting of fine paintings, and both in their love of great literature.

Later she wrote to him and told him that she was still not accustomed to their separation. There was much too much sobriety when he was gone; no one joked like he did. She went on to explain that they did not have much poetry at home, "father having made up his mind that it's pretty much all real life. Father's real life and mine sometimes come into collision, but as yet, escape unhurt." Emily's real life consisted of poetry, laughter, and sharing jokes with her siblings. Edward, stern and dignified, could never share their need for laughter.

In 1852, Edward was elected to Congress. Since that meant he would be away from home more, Austin decided his own place was closer to home. This decision, of course, pleased the entire family.

Emily wrote many of her letters in pencil. A pencil could be sharpened and used whenever she was ready. A pen had to be dipped in ink and would only write a few words before it had to be dipped again. When Emily had a thought she wanted to write down, she didn't want to have to wait. Her father wrote in ink. He sent to Boston for a special brand that he used with his quill pen. He used sand instead of blotting paper to dry the ink when he was finished.

Ink was expensive, and people who could not afford to buy it made their own. They would boil an ounce of logwood chips in a gallon of water for an hour or two, then strain the mixture. To that they would add nut galls, ground coarse; purified copperas: acetate of copper; pulverized sugar; and gum arabic. This was all brought to a boil, then set aside until it acquired the desired blackness. Then the ink could be strained and bottled for use with homemade quill pens.

U. S. postage stamps first appeared in 1847 and pictured Benjamin Franklin, the first postmaster general, and George Washington, the first president. They were not widely used until 1860. Instead, the postmaster used a large hand-cut stamp to stamp the mail when it was brought to him. Before the use of envelopes, the paper was folded to the proper size for mailing and sealed with wax. When Edward was elected representative to the 23rd Congress, he "franked" his letters. This was a mark affixed by special privilege to a letter or package, to ensure free transmission. The word "free" was part of the postmark, but outside of the circle.

The government had originally decided that the postal rate be based on the distance a letter was to travel. For instance, in 1835, the rate to send a letter from Amherst to Cincinnati, Ohio, was 25¢.

On March 3, 1845, Congress fixed the rates for a letter one-half ounce or less, at 5¢ for under 300 miles (480 km) and 10¢ for more than that, plus added costs for each additional half-ounce. By March 3, 1853, the rates for letters were 3¢ for under 3,000 miles (4,800 km) and 10¢ for over 3,000 miles, and they all had to be prepaid.

There were lots of letters lost in the mail and many complaints against postmasters, who were appointed on the basis of political consideration.

For example, they might get the job as a reward for supporting a congressman or for building up a party organization. They did not have to have any other qualifications.

This practice was continued until President James A. Garfield was shot and killed in 1881 by a man who thought he should have gotten a government job. There was not a specific job promised, but the man felt that some easy position should be found for him. There was widespread public outrage over the trivial reason for the death of the president, and in 1883, the Pendleton Act was passed that resulted in civil service reform. Slowly but steadily, federal jobs were dispensed not by patronage but based on the merit system.

In the meantime, many letters were carried by friends or acquaintances going in the direction of the letter. It was a lot more reliable. They were marked "to" followed by the person's name the letter was for, and "care of" followed by the name of the person who was carrying it as a favor.

Chapter

❖ SIX ❖

The social life of young people consisted of taffy pulls, playing charades, and sleigh rides. There was also a Shakespeare reading club. The leader of the club wanted to delete what he considered to be offensive pages. The male members of the club agreed. The young women, however, insisted on reading the complete, unexpurgated works.

There were also P.O.M. meetings. These were supposed to be poetry readings, but actually they were a chance for the young people to dance. They didn't tell their parents that P.O.M. stood for Poetry of Motion. Emily Fowler, Noah Webster's grand-daughter, often had them at her house. They were even more fun because the youths knew they were doing something frowned upon by the adults.

Emily and Austin hosted the meeting once when their parents were away. They all forgot to watch the hour until it was almost time for their parents to return home. In a flurry of activity, they managed to get everything back in place—almost everything. Their mother noticed that the lion rug on the hearth was upside down. Somehow she was persuaded not to "bother Father with it." But, after so close a call, Austin and Emily did not play host again to the P.O.M.

Vain amusements were forbidden to the Puritan Congregationalists. No organized sports were played, and gymnastics were considered a frivolity. Moderation in all things was the rule, except for hard work. The evenings the young people spent together were always chaperoned by parents. There were no street lights, only an occasional oil lamp above a gate; they were not considered necessary. A nine o'clock bell tolled every night to inform citizens that it was time for bed.

Vinnie was home from her school, having finished the requirements her father deemed necessary. She knew of Emily's friendship with Ben Newton and she was there to console her when Emily read in the *Springfield Republican* that Ben had died of consumption on March 24, 1853. Ben was one of the first of Emily's close friends to die. It weighed heavily on her mind and in her heart. Her cousin, Emily Norcross, had died the year before. This death did not seem to disturb Emily as much, probably because even though they had roomed together and were cousins, they were mentally and spiritually incompatible.

Austin was away at Harvard getting his law degree. He had decided that teaching was not for him. Emily wrote him often and hinted about her feelings over Newton's death.

Not all her letters to him were sad. She told him of the great delight Edward took in getting letters from Austin, how he read them over and over, "as if it were a blessing to have an only son." Emily told him how their father would get the family's letters at the post office and open them all, no matter who they were addressed to, so anxious was he to hear from Austin. Later, he would have Emily read them aloud at the supper table. Then, later in the evening, he would crack some walnuts, put on his spectacles, and sit down to read the latest letter once more.

"I believe at this moment, Austin," she wrote, "that there is nobody living for whom father has such respect as for you." This was probably true, and no one loved Austin more than his sister, Emily. But at the same time it must have been a thorn in her side to know that no matter what she did, Austin was and always would be the heir apparent. Edward was the sovereign, Austin the crown prince, and the rest of the family were but extensions of the lives of the men.

On May 9, 1853, Amherst celebrated the opening of the Amherst and Belchertown railroad. At last there was an alternative to the stagecoach. Emily did not join in the celebration but watched it from a field nearby. She did not want to be around the crowds. Later in the day, the celebration moved to the mansion. Her father had been instrumental in getting the railroad built; it was really a day for him as much as for the village. The women provided the refreshments for everyone. Emily was glad when they came. She finally got to meet Dr. Holland and his wife, Elizabeth, in person for the first time.

Emily and Dr. Holland had been exchanging

letters since he had published her valentine in 1852. He praised the poems she sent to him and occasionally sent her one of his to read.

She and Vinnie were invited to visit them in Springfield. The times that they did go, Emily was very happy. She felt that it was a warm "second home" to her. Dr. Holland treated her as a fellow writer and told her he had great admiration for her talent.

That Thanksgiving, Austin and Sue Gilbert announced their engagement. The entire family was very happy. Emily told Sue that she was glad that Sue would truly be her sister now.

Emily and Vinnie were considered adults, with adult responsibilities. But in their own home, they were still the children. Their mother believed that home should be a pleasant place for the children, so that they would always choose the kinds of peaceful and purifying activities that went on at home. Their achievements were minimized, especially in public, to prevent vanity. However, Emily's parents did not believe in continuous faultfinding. They felt it was better to express pleasure at good than displeasure at bad. They hoped by their own examples to show their children the right way to live.

Emily said that her mother "did not care for thought." It is possible that her mother did not have much time for thought. Her life was set to follow a pattern that did not allow for much free time.

Free time meant that something was left undone. Their religion taught that idle hands were the work of the Devil. The lamps had to be cleaned daily and refilled with whale oil. The water pitchers for every bedroom had to be filled each day from the kitchen pump, and the feather beds had to be made.

Vinnie did the marketing daily for the family and went to the post office when Edward was away. Their mother and Emily continued the daily tasks at home while she was gone, awaiting her return to find out the news of the day. If there was a new baby in town or any other event requiring a social visit, their mother would call on the family with appropriate gifts of food or flowers from the garden.

A washerwoman would come in for a day once a week. She would fill the boiler from the pump and heat the water on the stove. The clothes would then be boiled for an hour with homemade laundry soap before being scrubbed. The sadirons were heated on the stove, and the ironing would begin as the clothes were brought in off the line. If the clothes were too dry, they had to be dampened again before the ironing began. At different times, there were two different women, both named Maggie, who helped with the housework. They did whatever was needed around the house, but there were never enough hands to do all the work.

Cleanliness, it was believed, was next to godliness. Floors had to be swept with a broom daily and washed. The dust raised by the sweeping had to be wiped from the furnishings. More and more of the burden of daily life fell to Emily and Vinnie, as their mother's health did not allow her to do it.

Their parents realized the load the girls were carrying and appreciated it. However, they could not praise them that much, as it was expected of them. But they did try in other ways to show their love. They encouraged the girls to make trips to visit friends.

Edward was still very much involved in politics. In 1853, while serving as the state representative from the 10th Congressional District of Massachusetts, he had to spend time away from home. It was a good time, he felt, for the family to visit Washington.

Emily decided to stay at home. Susan Gilbert and Emily's cousin, John Graves, stayed with her for company and protection. The protection was as much from gossip as it was from worry about physical harm. It was unheard of for a decent, respectable single woman in those days to stay alone in a house.

Susan went to bed one evening while Emily and John stayed in the parlor talking. Emily soon decided to play some of her music, melodies she had made up herself. John was enchanted with her playing, but it woke Sue up and she let Emily know that it didn't enchant her. She wanted to get some sleep!

Emily kept up with the controversy in Congress over the Kansas–Nebraska Bill. Edward favored the definite restrictions against slavery north of the line laid down in the Missouri Compromise and opposed giving the settlers the right to decide the slavery question for themselves. When the Kansas–Nebraska Bill passed, Edward sensed that it meant the end of the Whig party, which stood strongly behind the Missouri Compromise, and he met with about twenty other Congressmen and agreed that the only hope lay in a new party, to be called the Republican party. Edward's career as a Whig was over.

Emily was interested, but other things took up more of her mind and her heart. Ben Newton's death continued to bother her. On January 13, 1854, Emily wrote to Unitarian minister Edward Everett Hale, Ben's pastor and a writer. She had to know if his last hours were cheerful and if he was willing to die. This was not an unusual question for the times. The threat of death was always lingering somewhere nearby.

Ben's death had caused Emily to have more doubts and questions about her religion. Her puritanical honesty, along with her inquiring mind, kept her examining what she knew of life and death and God's relationship to people.

Friendship, nature, and death were the favorite subjects of her poems. After Newton died, she seemed to become obsessed with death. Her cousin, William Norcross, brother of Emily Norcross, died in 1854 from the consumption that took so many members of that family.

In 1854, Emily's friendship with Sue almost ended. Sue could be very pushy, and she tried to force the usually sweet, cooperative Emily into converting, confessing her faith, and joining the church. Emily finally had enough. She wrote a note to Sue telling her that she could go or stay (in Emily's life), but that Emily could not honestly declare her faith, and if the friendship depended upon it, that friendship would end. Sue directed her efforts elsewhere after that.

On September 6, 1854, General David Mack died. This meant that the Dickinson homestead, purchased by him in 1833, would be on the market. Emily's father, being the oldest child of Emily's grandfather Samuel, had felt it was his duty to recoup the family fortune and turn Samuel's failures into successes. He had worked hard at his law practice and as treasurer of the college, and had paid back the debts incurred by his father. Now he could do the final act to redeem his family's name. He could buy back the old homestead and move his family into it, where he felt they belonged. He began to take the steps necessary to buy the mansion.

In February and March of 1855, Emily went with her family to Washington. They all stayed at the Willard Hotel. Emily charmed her father's friends and colleagues with her wit and insight.

Thomas D. Eliot, also a member of Congress, was staying at the same hotel with his family. He was very affectionate with his daughters, and he kissed them all good night. Vinnie, observing this one night, turned to Emily and said, "Father never kissed us good night in his life. He would die for us, but he would die before he would let us know it." Emily smiled at the thought of her father kissing her or her brother or sister—or even her mother. But she never doubted that they were all loved.

She and Vinnie also saw an old friend, Helen Fiske, now Helen Hunt. She had attended Abbott's Institute in New York and then married Lieutenent Edward B. Hunt in 1852. He was an army engineer, and Emily found him fascinating. They thought the same way about so many things. He said that she was "uncanny." When they parted, he told her he was sure he would see her again.

In March, Emily and Vinnie left Washington and went to Philadelphia, where they stayed with Eliza Coleman for two weeks. Eliza still had consumption. It had killed her sister, Olivia, but it was developing more slowly in her. She would eventually marry and have children before her death at age forty.

Emily met the Reverend Charles Wadsworth while visiting Eliza in Philadelphia. The first time she heard him, she was at the Arch Street Presbyterian Church. As a pulpit orator, his reputation was equaled only by Henry Ward Beecher, and he obviously had a deep sense of conviction. She later sought, through letters, his spiritual guidance.

She would not compromise her honesty and accept certain dogmas and interpretations of the Orthodox Congregational Church. She alienated many friends who joined the church. They did not understand that she was only seeking to find the truth.

On April 20, 1855, a notice in the *Express* told that Deacon Mack's home had been sold by his son, Samuel E. Mack of Cincinnati, to the honorable Edward Dickinson. Since Emily had felt so torn when they had moved from the mansion, it was thought that she would be pleased by the news. This was not the case. She had grown accustomed to the Pleasant Street home, and moving again once more meant leaving a part of herself behind.

However, she was delighted to find that Edward had offered to build a new house for Austin and Sue right near the mansion. This meant that the family would remain close to each other. Austin had graduated from Harvard Law School and had been admitted to the Hampshire County Bar in 1854. Now he would be going into his father's firm as a partner. Other things might change, but the Dickinsons were going to stay together.

Chapter

❖ SEVEN ❖

There was a lot of work to be done on the mansion before the family could move back into it. Many improvements were made, such as a water pump and sink in the kitchen. A cupola and two more chimneys were added. Edward also had one thing done just for Emily. He had a glass conservatory added to the house for her plants and flowers. It opened off the dining room and was lined with white shelves.

The mansion was cleaned thoroughly before the family moved into it. The furnishings were cleaned at the old house before they were moved. All the carpets were taken outside and beaten with a rug beater. When the beds were taken apart to be moved, they were not only cleaned but the ropes that stretched back and forth across the bedsteads to hold the mattresses were checked and replaced if needed.

Emily's mother fell into a deep, mystifying depression on the return to the mansion. Emily and Vinnie had to manage all the household activities plus tend to their mother in case she wanted or needed anything.

After they finished moving, Emily wrote to Mrs. Holland: "I cannot tell you how we moved. . . . I took at the time, a memorandum of my several senses, and also of my hat and coat, and my best shoes—but it was lost in the mêlée, and I am out with lanterns, looking for myself."

In the same letter she told Mrs. Holland that Mrs. Dickinson had been an invalid since the return to the mansion, and she and Vinnie had to manage everything and get settled while their mother laid on the lounge or sat in her easy chair. Emily didn't understand her mother's illness.

The family had taken special care that their piece trunk had not been lost in the move. Every home had piece trunks or drawers that held odds and ends—bits of dress fabric, ribbons, laces, flowers, feathers (kept in boxes), and so on—that had been taken off old hats and other clothing items and would be used on new ones.

Most clothing was homemade. The men sometimes had a tailor for their suits, but collars, shirt "bosoms" (the front part of a shirt that showed when a suit was worn), the high old-fashioned stocks (a bandlike collar or neckcloth), and neckties, shirts, and fancy waistcoats were made at home. Doeskin vestings, cassimeres (a twillweave worsted suiting fabric), black and figured silks, satins, damasks, and grenadines (thin-weave fabrics of silk or wool) were staples in the general store, as was the broadcloth that Edward always wore.

A seamstress generally came in for a day to cut and fashion dresses, but the needlework was done by the women in the family. They sewed fine seams by hand, as well as adding bits and pieces of decoration from the piece trunk.

The dresses were lined and reinforced with whalebone, thin strips of stiffening, each of which was covered before being sewn into the lining. For undergarments, triple seams were sewn for added strength and wear.

This was also the era of the hoop skirt. By 1859, the Douglas and Sherwood factory on White Street in New York was in full production. The 800 women they employed used 200 sewing machines to make 3,000 hoop skirts per day. Seamstresses all around the country had to keep up with fashion and be able to design dresses to fit over these hoops. Their advertisements in *Harper's Weekly* assured the wearer of their hoops' safety, comfort, and elegance. The matinee skirt had eleven hoops that could be detached to wash the skirt, and an adjustable bustle. This was supposed to eliminate any danger of entangling the feet or a foreign substance in the hoops.

Clothing was worn for years and years. It was well cared for and carefully mended when necessary. When fashions changed, the clothing was sometimes taken apart and the cloth reused for the new fashions. Stockings were knitted by the women and darned by hand when they got holes in them. This was in part for economy, but even when they could afford to have new, it went against the Puritan ethic of frugality and self-denial to buy a new item when the old could be repaired.

Edward was as stern with himself as he was with others; yet, in his own way, he was generous with his family. He knew they would not abuse what he gave them.

There was a new amusement among the young ladies. They began to ride horseback for fun, using sidesaddles. Riding clothes were different from ordinary dress. They had to be made in such a manner as to make it easy to mount and dismount from the saddle. The lady's right knee was wrapped around the pommel while riding, so that both legs were on the horse's left side. Riding astride was for men only. Dismounting was hazardous, as the voluminous drapery a woman was compelled to wear while riding could easily catch on some projection and cause injury or, perhaps even worse, a social embarrassment.

On July 1, 1856, Austin and Sue were married in Geneva, New York. None of the Dickinsons attended, possibly because Emily's mother was still deep in her apathy, and they would not add the strain of a wedding to her troubles. But they were ready to welcome Sue as part of the family when she and Austin returned.

Sue finally had a family—the most prominent one in Amherst—plenty of friends, and a new home called the Evergreens. She only had to cross a yard and walk through the hemlock hedge to get to the mansion, and there was a path worn between the two places before long. Emily could sit at her bedroom window and see Austin and Sue's home.

In August, Lt. Edward Hunt, Helen Fiske Hunt's husband, attended a meeting of the American Association for the Advancement of Science in Providence, Rhode Island. It was an annual meeting that he always attended and prepared a

The Evergreens

paper for. On the way home, he stopped to discuss the meeting with Emily.

He and Emily were much the same. They both hated trivialities, gossip, and petty arguments. Like Emily, he refused to affiliate himself with any church, as he disliked the narrowing effects of theologians on the mind.

He thought that science brought deeper and clearer insight and an ever expanding faith in the Lord as "Designing Author." These thoughts echoed Emily's in many ways. What she knew and learned from nature was at odds with the organized religion she knew.

He recognized her unusual mind, her charm, and her wit. His mind, in turn, was strong enough and rich enough to meet hers. She corresponded with him from that time. He may have been one of her so-called Masters.

There were at least three letters written to someone Emily called "Master." No one knows who they were to, if they were all to one person, or even if they were ever sent. They are love letters, beseeching the recipient to return her love and to understand her and her poetry. She seems to realize that the love she seeks is unattainable, and the letters become quite poignant.

The letters could have been, like much of her poetry, simply the artist at work, trying her hand and pen at the words of love to a phantom lover only she could see. If they were to a real person, there are many possibilities as to who this person could have been.

The families soon settled into everyday life. The endless work was still there in addition to her mother's more frequent bouts of illness. In September, Mrs. Dickinson went to Dr. Denniston's Hydropathic Institute in Northampton for the "water cure," but it didn't work. The warm natural mineral waters, which were both drunk and bathed in, were supposed to cure all kinds of illnesses.

Emily often slipped through the hedge by the narrow path she said was "just wide enough for two who love," to visit Sue. Sue kept the most widely discussed current literature in her home, both books and magazines. She had traveled more than most of the people in Amherst. Her upbringing had been rather different. Her first Christmas in Amherst, she upset the Dickinson family when she put laurel wreaths in the windows. They thought that only Catholics did things like that! However, Squire Dickinson supported Sue's actions, so no one said anything to her. Every Sabbath morning after she and Austin were married, Edward would cross the yards and enjoy a strong cup of coffee with her.

Emily would snatch precious minutes from the day to write a line or two when a poem came into her head. She would write on scraps of paper, such as the backs of old shopping lists, not only because they were handy when she was working around the house but also because of the frugality she had been taught.

The first note she sent across the yards to Sue at the Evergreens said:

One sister have I in our house
And one a hedge away—
There's only one recorded
But both belong to me.

One came down the road that I came—
And wore my last year's gown—
The other, as a bird her nest,
Builded our hearts among.[1]

Emily did feel like she had gained a sister, since she had loved her as one even before Sue's marriage to Austin. Sue learned that Emily, sweet and calm on the outside, had an iron will, and no amount of pushing on Sue's part would ever change her. Emily, in turn, accepted Sue's very outgoing personality and in some ways lived vicariously through Sue.

Since ladies did not go out much unless they were escorted, and Emily's mother was becoming frailer all the time, more and more Emily abandoned the social life of the village. Even when she did go to church, the other people stared at her and made her uncomfortable. She was never sure if it was because they didn't see her very often or because they all knew she hadn't converted.

Sue had a quick mind and was able to converse with Emily on a level she had been used to with her family. If the Dickinsons had always been atypical, Sue was just as atypical and fit in well. This did not mean that she was like them. She was different from them in many ways. Also, she was much more social and loved to entertain.

Sue delighted in the gaiety and conversation that accompanied the dinner parties she hosted. She often had distinguished guests and lively en-

[1] Polly Longsworth, *Emily Dickinson: Her Letters to the World*, (New York: Thomas Y. Crowell Company, 1965).

tertainment. Once, after Ralph Waldo Emerson had lectured at Amherst College, he stayed at the Evergreens as a guest. Emily sent Sue a note saying, "It must have been as if he had come from where dreams are born."

The library at the mansion was well used. Emily had her favorite books. She called them her "kinsmen of the shelves." There were books by John Keats, John Ruskin, William Shakespeare, and Charles Dickens, as well as others. The Bible was a major source of poetic inspiration for Emily, especially the Book of Revelations.

She enjoyed the work of her contemporaries, like the novels of George Eliot and the poems of Elizabeth Barrett Browning and her husband, Robert. *Godey's Lady Book* advised the perfect hostess to separate the male and female authors on her bookshelves.

Edward still objected to some of the books Emily read. One morning he saw her reading Herman Melville while she was cooking breakfast. He didn't say anything to her then, but later he read aloud from the Bible the parable of the servant who buried the gold given him by his master rather than putting it to profitable use.

Twice a day he would lead the family in prayers and read a chapter of the Bible aloud. Life was synonymous with duty—civic, moral, religious, and so on—all to be shouldered and carried out to the best of one's ability.

George Eliot, pseudonym
of Mary Ann Evans Cross

There was a cattle show every year in Amherst. It was much like a county fair. Emily entered some of her bread and won first prize on May 26, 1857. Her father, of course, had been confident of her winning. Hadn't he always said hers was the best? He would never brag to his friends nor praise her in front of them, but she knew that he was pleased when the judges agreed with what he had said all along.

The *Atlantic Monthly* started publication in Boston in November. The Dickinsons were charter subscribers. This literary magazine's first issue contained "The Maple," a sonnet by the editor-in-chief, James Russell Lowell; an essay and four poems by Ralph Waldo Emerson; and stories by Henry Wadsworth Longfellow, Harriet Beecher Stowe, John Townsend Trowbridge, and others. Oliver Wendell Holmes initiated a series of personal essays in the magazine under the title, "The Autocrat of the Breakfast Table." In later issues, the other writers were joined by Thomas Wentworth Higginson, who became the most frequent, if least famous, writer for the magazine. By April of 1862, twenty-two essays by Higginson had appeared in the magazine.

The year 1858 was the beginning of the most creative period of Emily's life. She wrote over fifty poems that year and drafted her first "Master" letter. She still devoted some of her time to a social life. She was asked to be a judge in the bread

Elizabeth Barrett Browning

division of the cattle show that year and she accepted. Naturally, she found time to visit next door. Austin had a mild case of typhoid fever in October 1858 and it scared the whole family. There was no cure for typhoid fever then. He finally got well.

Austin had met Samuel Bowles, the editor of the *Springfield Republican,* and became friends with him. Sam's father had gone up the Connecticut River from Hartford in true pioneer style, with his wife, baby, and printing press all on a flatboat. He brought out the first issue of the *Springfield Republican* on September 8, 1824. Sam became the owner and editor after his father's death from dysentery in 1851. Emily, of course, already knew Josiah Holland, the literary editor of the paper. Sam came to the Evergreens to visit and occasionally, in the beginning, he brought his wife with him. Emily met them on one of their visits.

Sam was intelligent, enthusiastic, and had a quick imagination. His newspaper was one of the foremost in the nation. He admired Emily and enjoyed her company. However, his health was frail, and he had to guard against overextending himself. He had neither the time nor the strength to give Emily the intensive relationship she wanted. He did write to her, and whenever he did, he called her his "Queen Recluse."

That Bowles and Holland were friends with Emily is rather amazing. They held many of the same opinions of women as their contemporaries. They were tolerant but condescending. In fact, both printed essays in the *Republican* outlining their views about educated women. One that appeared on December 6, 1865, said that there was a surplus of teachers, and employment prospects for women were discouraging. Another possible career was authorship, but the editors didn't like this. They said the women usually wrote flowery manuscripts and watered-down imitations of Thackeray.

They claimed that a large class of young people, mostly women, wrote to console themselves for sorrows real or imaginary, and they had no respect for the young women of the day who thought they were unappreciated. They thought these women should be put to work at some useful domestic occupation, until such thoughts were driven out of them and they would do their daily tasks without sulking.

They were rash in their essays about women, but they published women's poetry because it sold papers. No matter what Emily did, she could not really get help from either of them. If she wrote for the public, she was not writing the strong verse she was capable of. If she wrote the way she felt, it would not be understood or "fit in" with the poetry of the times.

Early in 1860, Emily was visited by the Reverend Charles Wadsworth, whom she had met in Philadelphia. Until that year, her poems were about life, death, nature, and self-knowledge. After this, they changed to love—love that bloomed, became blighted, and finally resigned itself to being unrequited.

Edward read about the Lincoln–Douglas debates in the *Republican* but refused to take Abraham Lincoln seriously. He called Lincoln "just a local politician" and felt that all the ranting about a "house divided" did more harm than good. He thought that minor politicians like Lincoln would drop by the wayside, and then the slavery issue would just quietly work itself out. However, in 1860, Abraham Lincoln was elected president. South Carolina seceded from the Union in protest. In his inaugural address in 1861, the new president warned the South that secession was illegal, and he was willing to use force to preserve the Union.

Emily read the newspaper accounts of the slavery issue, which was becoming more and more pressing. When John Brown captured the federal arsenal at Harpers Ferry in a plot to liberate the slaves, then was caught and sentenced to death, she was grieved. She believed in the abolitionist cause, as she believed in freedom for all, but she couldn't accept violence as a solution. However, she was even more upset over the recent death of Elizabeth Barrett Browning, one of her idols. Emily had read Browning's *Aurora Leigh*, which had been published in 1857 as a nine-book, blank-verse romance. It was about the philosophic and romantic adventures of an aspiring and eventually successful female poet. The book was condemned in Boston as the "hysterical indecencies of an erotic mind."

Emily was too busy to remain depressed for long, especially with the news from next door. She was to become an aunt! Austin and Sue were finally beginning their family.

On May 4, Emily's "The May Wine" was published in the *Springfield Republican*. Her words seem to give a feeling of joy at being alive. These words are in direct contrast to the "Master" letters she was drafting at the time.

> *I taste a liquor never brewed,*
> *From tankards scooped in pearl;*
> *Not all the vats upon the Rhine*
> *Yield such an alcohol!*

Inebriate of air am I,
And debauchee of dew,
Reeling, through endless summer days,
From inns of molten blue.

When landlords turn the drunken bee
Out of the foxglove's door,
When butterflies renounce their drams,
I shall but drink the more!

Till seraphs swing their snowy hats,
And saints to windows run,
To see the little tippler
Leaning against the sun![2]

These lines do not seem to reflect the grief of unrequited love that she writes of in her letters.

She tried to spend more time with Sue. Pregnancy was still treated as an illness. There were no cesarian operations, and no anesthetics. Very primitive instruments were usually used when there was a difficult birth, instruments that were dangerous to mother and child. At any sign of illness in the expectant mother, she was bled. Sometimes several quarts of her blood would be removed in a two-day period.

Expectant women did not go out in public, but this did not prevent other women from visiting them and regaling them with tales of horror about their own difficult deliveries or ones they had heard of in which both mother and child had died.

Sue was on the verge of hysteria most of the time. Emily's calm presence seemed to comfort her. Austin was no help, as anything and everything

[2] Martha Dickinson Bianchi and Alfred Leete Hampson, eds., *The Poems of Emily Dickinson* (Boston: Little, Brown and Company, 1944).

having to do with childbirth was left strictly to the women. Men and women did not even discuss it together.

Sam Bowles sent Sue a copy of Dickens' *Great Expectations* when it was published this same year. The title by itself amused Sue, considering her condition, but the book itself was also greatly appreciated by her as it helped her to pass the time with one of the family's favorite authors.

The Governor and Mrs. Banks were house guests at the mansion. They spent three nights there and left on August 11, 1860. Lt. Edward Hunt and his wife, Helen, were in Amherst during August and September and attended a reception given for the Bankses at the mansion.

There was quite a stir in town when a sealed box arrived addressed to the treasurer of Amherst College from David Sears of Boston. It had instructions with it that it should not be opened for one hundred years on pain of forfeiture of the gift it contained.

David Sears was one of the richest men in New England. He had given $10,000 to the troubled college in the early 1840s. He had never visited Amherst but had been impressed with the actions of the faculty under President Hitchcock when they agreed to donate their services to rescue the college from financial ruin. Between 1844 and 1850, Sears added securities and two pieces of Boston real estate (both of which were later sold) to establish the Sears Fund of Literature and Benevolence.

Chapter

EIGHT

On June 19, 1861 (the year the Civil War broke out), Sue gave birth to a boy. He wasn't named right away, but the family called him "Union Jack." The Dickinsons finally became concerned that he would never be called anything else if they didn't do something about a "real" name soon.

Waiting to name a child was a custom that was widespread in New England. One after another, children would be born and live only long enough to make losing them more painful. Because of this, often there was no formal acknowledgement of the birth until the child had weathered the dangers of the first few months of life. Sometimes, they were not named until they were a year old. Many died before they were officially named.

Later in the year, Sue and Austin sent a note across the yards to the mansion. It was supposed to be a message from Jackey to his grandfather. In the note, he said that his mother liked the name of his grandfather, and he wondered if he might have one just like it.

Jackey got an answer on December 6, 1861. His grandfather consented to Jackey having a name just like his. So the baby was named Edward, nicknamed Ned. Young Edward was adored by his entire family. Emily was enchanted with the little boy and went to see him often.

In December of 1861, the telegraph came to Amherst. It was the wonder of the day. Imagine, sending messages over wires! How exciting that words could race through them and not have to wait for the mail!

Greater communications with the outside world brought an even greater interest in cultivating the social graces in Amherst. Sue became an important participant in the changing scene. She was called the social leader of the day, a highly cultivated woman of great taste and refinement. However, it was also said that she was a little too aggressive and sharp-witted to deserve great social prestige.

Austin was not comfortable with his wife's high society tactics, but he was not idle in community life either. He organized the village improvement society, supervised the building of a new church, and moderated at town meetings. If anything concerned Amherst, Austin was involved.

In 1862, Emily seemed to have had a severe emotional crisis. Possibly it was due to Charles Wadsworth moving to California, where he had accepted a call to the Calvary Church in San Francisco, or perhaps it was because Sam Bowles left on a trip to Europe and Emily could no longer count on seeing him or getting letters from him on a regular basis. For whatever reason, Emily began to feel very much alone, deserted by her closest friends.

On March 1, Emily's poem "The Sleeping" was published in the *Springfield Republican*. On April 15, Emily wrote to Col. Thomas Higginson seeking literary advice. Higginson was a radical Unitarian minister in Newburyport, Massachusetts, from 1847 to 1852. He was also an abolitionist (opposed to slavery). Twice he tested the new Fugitive Slave Law in Boston, once by a conspiracy that failed in 1851 and again in 1854 by conspiracy and violence. Anthony Burns, a fugitive slave, had run away from slavery in Virginia where he was a Baptist preacher. He made his way to Boston, where he was arrested and confined to jail in the courthouse. All of Boston was in an uproar. Thomas Higginson was one of the abolitionists who led an excited crowd to the courthouse and started to batter the door down with a heavy timber to rescue Burns. The plot failed, and Higginson received a deep cut in the chin when the police surged in. Burns, judged a fugitive, was sent back to Virginia.

The episode was covered and applauded by the *Springfield Republican*. Higginson belonged to the Secret Six who conspired with John Brown in planning the Harpers Ferry raid on October 16, 1859. This event was also reported in the newspaper.

In the fall of 1862, during the Civil War, Higginson was given command of the first black regiment. He also held the rank of Lieutenant Colonel as he led the 29th regiment. He was referred to as "Colonel" from then on.

Col. Higginson read the poems Emily sent him. He was embarrassed by his inability to classify them.

Colonel Thomas W. Higginson

He thought they were "remarkable, though odd," but not publishable. The public wanted their poetry to be like all the other poetry at that time, and hers, he told her, violated literary convention. On June 8, 1862, Emily wrote back to him, "I smile when you suggest that I delay to publish, that being as foreign to my thoughts as firmament to fin."

She continued in the letter to agree with him on his perception of her work, but in a mocking way. At the end, she asked him to be her preceptor (teacher). He agreed, and she sent him more of her work. However, she was not honest with him as far as the number of poems she had written. She let him think she had just started writing, when in reality she had already written hundreds of poems.

By June, Emily began her almost total withdrawal from society. She was comfortable at home. The familiar environment felt safe to her. This is about the time that she started to wear only white dresses, summer and winter. They were made of mens' formal shirting fabric of embossed cotton. No one knows why she did this. Possibly it was because they represented the purity and simplicity she was trying to express in her life and her poetry. Possibly it was because of her religious beliefs. Wearing any apparel that decorated the body could be considered vanity. Whatever the reason, her decision made the people of the village think of her as being even more strange than they had before.

There were flags and drums and marching in the streets during the Civil War. The women got together to weave blankets and knit socks for the soldiers. Emily did not join them. She considered these to be more social occasions than work. She needed time to read and write.

She might have been more concerned with the war if her brother had had to go. But he bought a "substitute" for $500 to go in his place. This is what most of the wealthy did in those days. The person who went in their place was usually from a very poor family, and the money was more than they had ever seen at one time.

There were shortages during the war. Sorghum and maple sugar were used for sweetening, and the first experiments to extract sugar from beets were tried. Chicory seed was often used as a substitute for coffee. However, life went on as usual in many respects for a lot of people. In 1864, when the struggle was in its fourth year, an English visitor to Boston found no trace of the war worth recording. He was impressed with the solidity and stability of the country he saw. Those whose duty it was to fight, fought. The rest of the country carried on as they always had.

For Emily, that meant taking care of her mother. It appeared that she had no choice but to give up socializing. This was not difficult for her. Her friends had married and had children and she had nothing in common with them anymore. Emily Fowler had married Gordon Ford in 1853 and moved to Brooklyn, where she wrote a two-volume biography of her grandfather, Noah Webster. She also wrote essays, stories, and a book of verse, all of which were published.

Emily Dickinson thought that, for the most part, women had "muslin souls" and "dimity convictions." She had great respect for women such as Florence Nightingale and Elizabeth Barrett Browning, who made use of their talents. After the others were in bed for the night, Emily would stay up in her room writing at her desk. She had a ladies' writing table, 17.5 inches square, with one drawer. She wrote by the light of the oil lamp she kept there. She had portraits of Elizabeth Barrett Browning, George Eliot, Ralph Waldo Emerson, and Thomas Carlyle on her walls to keep her company throughout the dark hours.

Her family accepted her the way she was. They did not try to make her go out and socialize when she didn't want to. Vinnie, in particular, shielded her from the outside world. Vinnie continued to do all the marketing and any errands that had to be done in town. She covered for Emily by making excuses to other people as to why her sister was not going out. She wrote letters to the people that Emily didn't want to write to. She remembered to have the fruit and vegetables picked for canning and to save the seeds for the next year. And she was always there to graciously welcome any and all visitors to the mansion.

This does not mean that Emily forgot other people. She had a lot of empathy for them and kept up with what was going on by listening to Vinnie's stories. If there was an illness in a family, or a birth or death, Emily would send flowers from her own garden and many times an appropriate poem she had written.

Emily wrote many poems over and over again, trying to find just the right words. In her writing, she was also trying to find the answers to questions that had plagued her since she was old enough to question religion and its place in the world.

She thought about people such as Charlotte

Lavinia Dickinson

Brontë and wondered where the justice was. Charlotte had had so much talent and so much to give the world. She had refused marriage in 1839, saying that any man would be startled to see her natural character. He would think her a wild, romantic soul. She would not sit solemnly all day before her husband, which was expected of a decorous woman. Emily could relate to these feelings.

Twice more, Charlotte rejected suitors. Then, in 1852, she was wooed and won by Reverend Arthur Bell Nickols. She married him in 1854 but died a year later from complications of childbirth. Was this the reward for doing what society said was right? If so, to Emily, the reward was not worth the price.

Nor was it worth the price to have her work published and held before the public for criticism. In this era, any woman in the public eye was testing the limits that society had put upon her. It meant that she was inserting herself into the public affairs of men and deserting the private domestic sphere for which she was intended.

Those women who did cross the line usually tried to keep a low profile. For instance, Catharine Maria Sedgwick (1789–1867) was one of the first women to become commercially successful as a writer in her time. By 1830, she had written four novels and was earning a significant income but still claiming that she did not have an occupation. She never married—this at a time when a spinster was considered less of a woman—but lived in the homes of her brothers. Living by herself, which she could well have afforded, would have been too bold a move.

Caroline Lee Hentz (1800–1856) began writing

Catharine M. Sedgwick

when her husband became too ill to work. As the sole provider for her family, she produced fifteen volumes of fiction in less than ten years. She rationalized her writing and the success that came from it by claiming family need. This was a rationalization that society could accept.

Harriet Beecher Stowe (1811–1896) realized her potential for financial freedom when *Uncle Tom's Cabin* netted her $10,000 in the first three months of sales. She and her husband had seven children, and his income as a teacher, scholar, and clergyman did not provide adequately for the family. She became an active businesswoman and one of the few who did not apologize for her success.

Emily continued to read the newspapers and magazines. When she read of these women and what happened to most of them—how they often groveled at the feet of people who should be praising them instead of criticizing them—it made her more determined to remain unmarried, subservient to no man, and to remain an unpublished and unknown poet, answerable to no one.

Emily's own ideas concerning publication are written in one of her poems. Why she felt this way when one of her greatest pleasures was reading, we can only guess.

Publication is the auction
Of the mind of man,
Poverty be justifying
For so foul a thing.

Possibly,—but would we rather
From our garret go
White unto the White Creator,
Than invest our snow.

Harriet Beecher Stowe

Thought belongs to Him who gave it—
Then to him who bear
Its corporeal illustration.
Sell the Royal air
In the parcel,—be the merchant
Of the Heavenly Grace,
But reduce no human spirit
To disgrace of price![1]

On September 30, 1863, Edward Hunt was in an accident on board a ship. He died from his injuries on October 2, at the age of forty-one, and had a military funeral on October 5. He had been promoted to the rank of major. After this, Emily did not communicate with Helen for a long time.

Emily was not feeling well, but she continued her duties and her writing. On March 12, 1864, her poem, "My Sabbath" was published in the *Round Table*. On March 30, "Sunset" was published in the *Springfield Republican*. Either Sue or Samuel Bowles arranged for the publication of these poems without her knowledge. When they were published, they were changed by a well-meaning editor to comply with the convictions of the day as to how poetry was supposed to be written. It upset Emily to see the rhyme, meter, and punctuation of her verses changed.

Edward became concerned with Emily's health, and in April he took her to Boston and placed her under the care of a physician there. She stayed with her cousins, Louisa and Fannie Norcross. Her

---

[1] Martha Dickinson Bianchi and Alfred Leete Hampson, eds., *The Poems of Emily Dickinson* (Boston: Little, Brown and Company, 1944).

eyes were causing her serious problems, and she was suffering from nervous depression. The doctor took her pen away from her and forbade her to read or write. She was allowed only to dictate letters that her cousins would write for her or write short notes in pencil.

She returned home in August, but there was not much change. She had to return to Boston in 1865 for more treatments. She hated going out, as she had already begun her life as a recluse. These trips that she took, and the length of time she stayed away from her home and the security she knew there, showed how important her writing was to her. Losing her eyesight forever and not being able to read or write was the worse fate she could think of.

The photographs and paintings of the Dickinson family suggest that Emily and her sister and mother all suffered in varying degrees from exotropia, or walleye. This congenital disorder is often seen soon after birth. Characteristic problems are eyestrain, blurring of vision, difficulties with prolonged periods of reading, headaches, double vision, and extreme sensitivity to bright light. All of these occur only intermittently. The photographs do not show that trait in Austin, but letters from Boston suggest he had it, too, even to the point of having to rest his eyes frequently.

"The Snake" was published in the *Springfield Republican* on February 14, 1866. This may have been the cause of the deterioration of Emily's friendship with Sue. Emily had accepted Sue as her sister and trusted friend and showered her with over 300 poems, but Sue violated this trust by sending in this poem for publication without Emily's consent. They began to drift farther apart. This was not the first time Sue had done it, but she continued even knowing Emily's feelings. The poem was, however, one that people of that time could understand and appreciate.

A Narrow fellow in the grass
Occasionally rides;
You may have met him,—did you not?
His notice sudden is.

The grass divides as with a comb,
A spotted shaft is seen;
And then it closes at your feet
And opens further on.

He likes a boggy acre,
A floor too cool for corn.
Yet when a child, and barefoot,
I more than once, at morn,

Have passed, I thought, a whip-lash
Unbraiding in the sun,—
When stooping to secure it,
It wrinkled, and was gone.

Several of nature's people
I know, and they know me;
I feel for them a transport
Of cordiality;

But never met this fellow,
Attended or alone,
Without a tighter breathing,
And zero at the bone.[2]

[2] Bianchi and Hampson, eds., *The Poems of Emily Dickinson*, p. 65.

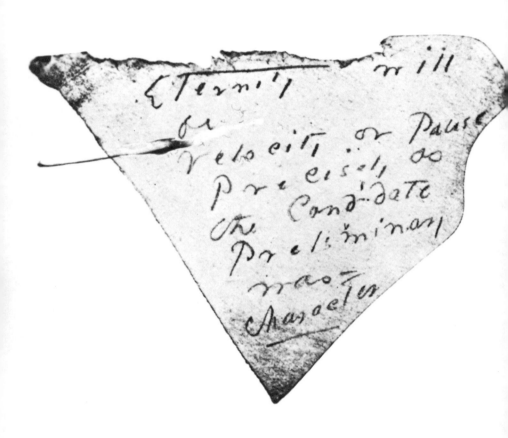

A scrap of Emily's writing,
on the flap of an envelope

This marks the end of Emily's most creative period. She had composed more than a thousand poems in eight years. All of them had been written in time snatched from other things, and most of them written by the light of a whale oil lamp while the rest of the household slept. This was very much like her grandfather Dickinson working until midnight and only allowing himself four hours of sleep a night.

Now those nights became even lonelier. The dog Carlo, her ever-faithful companion, had died.

Chapter

Sue and Austin became the parents of a baby girl on November 30, 1866. They named her Martha, but that was soon shortened to Mattie. Emily often babysat with Mattie when Austin and Sue went to church. They took Ned, but it was easier to leave the infant at home.

They quit trying to get Emily to go to church or anywhere else. They didn't understand her, but they did try to accept her as she was.

A handyman named Timothy was hired to do the heavier chores now. Austin was as busy as his father and could not do the things he had done as a boy. Timothy did work for both the homestead and the Evergreens. He would bring foaming pails of milk from the cows to the big house first. Emily would take out what they needed. She had to figure how much they would drink and how much she would need to make butter and still have enough cream for baking. The rest would be sent next door. Timothy would seldom just have the milk to take there. Often Emily would send magazines, cakes, or cookies along with a note or poem to Sue. Their relationship was not as close as it had been, but Emily still loved her brother and his children, and she would do anything she could to keep the family going.

Samuel Bowles was "Uncle Sam" to Sue and Austin's children. Through Sam, Sue and Austin became acquainted with Charles Dickens. When Sue and Austin had guests, even ones that Emily admired, it was never sure that she would come and join them. If she did, it would only be for a few moments. She craved the company of her peers yet was uneasy around other people.

Sam called her "part angel, part demon" when she refused to see him after he had driven over from Springfield just to see her. He yelled up the stairway at her and told her to come down. To the amazement of Vinnie, Emily did as she was told, and Emily and Sam had a nice visit.

He brought her manuscripts of famous writers before they were published. When he entertained Canon Kingsley, Bret Harte, Charles Dickens, or any other author of note, he shared his impressions of them with her.

The death of Charles Dickens in 1870 saddened Emily. She had enjoyed his writings. She had read his works when the first early installments came out in magazines, before they were printed in book form. She often read them to her nephew, Ned, and he enjoyed them as much as she did. They were not alone in mourning his loss. Everyone loved Dickens. When he gave his first reading in a theater in New York City in 1867, people had formed two lines almost a mile long waiting for the

ticket office to open. Ticket scalpers were getting $20 apiece for them.

Austin and Sue entertained Henry Ward Beecher, Governor Bullock, and Ralph Waldo Emerson in their home. A copy of *Essays and Poems* by Emerson was given to Emily, Sue, and Austin by Emerson himself. Emerson was perhaps the greatest influence on Emily as far as her poetry was concerned.

On August 16, 1870, Emily was visited by Col. Higginson. His visit renewed her poetic interests, and in the early 1870s she wrote nearly two hundred more poems.

Some of Emily's letters to Higginson reveal her feelings about the public in general. "Truth is such a rare thing, it is delightful to tell it," she says in one note. Later she asks him, "How do most people live without any thoughts? There are many people in the world—you must have noticed them in the street—how do they live? How do they get strength to put on their clothes in the morning?"

She seemed satisfied with her life as she was living it. Her own thoughts filled her mind and were joined with the thoughts of others whose writings she studied.

"There is no frigate like a book to take us lands away," she wrote. She felt that she could travel the world and meet all the people she wanted to through books. She never had to leave her own home, which she considered to be the best and safest place for her.

Charles Dickens

She did not concern herself with fashion. She thought that bustles, popular at this time, not only looked ridiculous but hampered women's movements as much or more than the hoop skirts had. The bustles were worn with long elaborate dresses that had puffed upper sleeves.

Helen Fiske Hunt's son Warren, known as Rennie, had died after a brief illness in the spring of 1865. Helen had gone into seclusion. Then she had decided to begin again, determined to become a writer. Early in 1866, she took two rooms in the select boarding house of Mrs. Dame in Newport, Rhode Island. Col. Higginson was residing there at the time, and she went to him for advice. She listened to what he told her and wrote in the manner that was accepted in that day and age, signing her work H.H. In less than two years, she was mentioned in his column on female poets of America.

Emily first saw a poem by H.H. in February 1869 in the *Atlantic Monthly*. A year after that, Helen was writing papers on domestic subjects for the *Independent* and other periodicals. She first published on her own a collection of her poems, *Verses by H.H.*; later it was published by Fields, Osgood and Company. She became the leading female poet of America.

Helen and Emily renewed their earlier friendship. Col. Higginson had shown some of Emily's poems to Helen. Helen visited Emily and tried to talk her into publishing some of them. She felt that

Helen Hunt Jackson

[110]

Emily was a genius and a far better poet than she, herself, and she wanted to help Emily. Emily refused to even consider publication.

Josiah Holland, after ending his association with the *Springfield Republican* in 1866, had taken his wife and three children abroad. After extended traveling, they returned to the States and launched *Scribner's Monthly*. It became the leading periodical of the 1870s. Based in New York, Dr. Holland was able to attract excellent writers, and he gave preference to American writers such as Bret Harte and Frank Stockton.

Col. Higginson visited Emily again on December 3, 1873. It would be the last time he would see her, though they did not know it at the time. He encouraged her to continue writing.

On June 16, 1874, Emily's father died. He had been delivering an address before the Massachusetts legislature favoring the proposed Hoosac Tunnel, later built to connect by rail the northwestern part of the state and the east. He suffered a stroke and was taken to his hotel room. A wire was sent to the family that he was gravely ill. Before Austin could finish harnessing the horse, the second message arrived saying that he had died.

Judge Otis Lord, an old family friend, tried to console the shocked Emily. Judge Lord might have been the lover Emily spoke of in her poetry. There is speculation, based on some of the letters she wrote to him, that they did have an affair. But, once again, Emily could have just been using words to express the fantasies of her mind. Many of her letters to both male and female were flowery and loving.

Judge Lord

Even with the help of Judge Lord, the death of her father may have been the final convincing argument for Emily. The world was an evil place, and no matter how you tried, the only answer to life was death. She entered complete seclusion.

This seclusion often went to dangerous extremes. Once, when she was ill, the doctor was called. He had to examine her as she walked past a doorway, basing his diagnosis on that short glimpse of her. In a letter she wrote to Col. Higginson concerning her father, she said "His heart was pure and terrible, and I think no other like it exists. . . ."

Later in the same letter: "I am glad there is Immortality, but would have tested it myself, before entrusting him."

These lines tell a lot about her feelings for her father and how deep they went. She not only meant that she would have liked to test death before him to smooth the way, but also because, if she had died first, she would not have to learn how to live without the man who was the major focal point of her and the rest of the family's lives.

No vacillating God
Ignited this abode
To put it out.

Those words show that Emily did believe in God and in life everlasting. Her beliefs were never based on any formal church but were possibly stronger than those of the "saved" who surrounded her.

There were no more family Thanksgiving dinners at the mansion after Squire Dickinson died. Without him there did not seem to be a reason to hold a celebration there.

Then another blow came. In June 1875, Emily's mother became paralyzed. She would be bedridden for the rest of her life. Emily had taken care of her for a long time, but not to the extent that it was now necessary. Her mother had to be bathed and fed and her linens changed regularly. Emily spent as much time with her mother as she could. Since Edward had died, she had more time. There was only herself and Vinnie in the house with their mother, and Vinnie did all the shopping and anything else that had to be done outside of the house.

Emily actually became closer to her mother after this illness struck. She never had much in common with her, but now her mother was the child and Emily was the adult. In many ways, her mother became the child that Emily never had.

There were other family problems. When Ned was fifteen, he developed epilepsy. At this time, epileptics were hidden from society. They were thought to be mentally ill, and people feared their attacks.

Sue, Ned's mother, could not cope with the attacks. She herself became prostrate whenever he had one. She felt guilty because while she had been expecting Ned, she remembered her sister, Mary, dying from complications of childbirth, and she knew that many women died giving birth. She had been afraid throughout the pregnancy and had even tried to abort the baby. She had had abortions previously because of her fears. Abortion was sometimes the only birth control available then. This time, the abortion didn't work, and she knew she would have to go through with the birth. She blamed herself and what she tried to do as the cause of Ned's epilepsy.

Austin had to take care of Ned during the attacks. He held him so that he couldn't hurt himself and pushed a spoon into his son's mouth to keep his tongue from going back into his throat and choking him. When the attacks were over, Ned fell into a deep sleep. He never remembered having had the attacks, and Austin never told him about them. Ned's illness caused a lot of marital problems between Sue and Austin.

Ned loved his Aunt Emily. He was never strong physically. He suffered from inflammatory rheumatism, and at the age of sixteen, he was left with a rheumatic heart. This kept him from contact sports, but he still liked to fish and ride, and he knew that Aunt Emily was always glad to see him and enter into a discussion of the latest books.

Judge Otis Lord visited Emily frequently. He gave her a shoulder to lean on and helped her through the trials that seemed to mount daily. He was one of the few people that Emily would see in person. By now, she was avoiding almost everyone. When anyone came to call, she would most often go upstairs, or into another room where she could listen but not be seen or have to talk if she didn't want to.

On August 1, 1875, Sue and Austin became parents for the third and last time. Thomas Gilbert, called Gil by his family, was born. He was a happy baby with a sunny disposition. Emily found time for Gil from the time he was born.

When he arrived, Ned was past twenty and Mattie was sixteen. He helped relieve the tensions between family members. Emily was glad of this because she wanted to keep the family intact, as it always had been.

Austin hoped that Gil would continue his family's name. Ned, never robust, had increasing periods of illness. He needed all his strength just to live. It was obvious by this time that neither Emily nor Vinnie would marry, and even if they had, the children's last names would not have been Dickinson. Now there was Gil, the heir that it was hoped would carry on the line.

Chapter

❖ TEN ❖

In 1873, Helen Hunt moved to Colorado Springs for her health. In 1875, she married W. S. Jackson, a banker. After living in the West for some time, she became intensely interested in American Indians and worked actively to better their living conditions.

Early in 1876, she was again urging Emily to write for publication. Emily, in turn, wrote to Col. Higginson and asked him to write Helen a note saying that he disapproved of her being published. Since Helen thought so highly of Col. Higginson, Emily felt that the note would stop Helen's crusade to have her poems published.

Either he didn't write the note or Helen ignored it. Helen could see, far better than Col. Higginson, the creative genius that was being hidden from the rest of the world.

That autumn, Dick, the new hired man at the mansion, lost a little girl to scarlet fever. Having taken over the job when Timothy quit, Dick had been at the mansion when the word came that Emily's father had died, and he had held Emily while she cried. Now she could do nothing to comfort him. The natural order of things is that a child will outlive the parent, but for a parent to watch a child die was something that went against nature. Emily felt helpless.

Possibly Emily regretted some of the decisions she had made. Whatever her reasons, she felt that she had chosen a life and that there was no turning back. In a note to Mattie, along with some choice flowers, she said, "Be sure to live in vain, dear. I wish I had." Emily thought others lived in vain, without real purpose in their lives. Her purpose to herself was her poetry. She probably felt at times that it would have been easier to live like other people. She didn't want Mattie to go through the same emotionally debilitating life she herself had led, but instead, to go into the world and live as others did.

In January 1878, Sam Bowles died. Austin and Vinnie went to the funeral, but Emily stayed home. She mourned in private just as she lived in private.

Around this time, Helen Hunt Jackson sent Emily's poem, "Success is Counted Sweetest," to Roberts Brothers Publishers.

Success is counted sweetest
By those who ne'er succeed.
To comprehend a nectar
Requires sorest need

Not one of all the purple host
Who took the flag today
Can tell the definition,
So clear, of victory,

As he, defeated, dying,
On whose forbidden ear
The distant strains of triumph
Break, agonized and clear.

The poem was published in *A Masque of Poets*. None
of the poets was identified in the book. The publisher thought it would be great fun for the public
to try to figure out who wrote what. Poets were
very popular, and each had his or her own style
that usually marked the works. It is not known if
Emily had given her permission to publish the
poem or not.

Mr. Thomas Niles of the literary department
became interested in the "new" poet (Emily). He
wrote to her, and they became friends through
their letters. He tried to induce her to publish what
she sent him privately. This is the same man that
told Louisa May Alcott, "Why don't you write a
story for girls?" Emily continued to write to him
but would not consent to be published.

On July 5, 1879, at 1:30 A.M., there was a big
fire in Amherst. The fire leapt from roof to roof
along the west side of the village green from
Amherst House to the post office and bank, then
to the town offices, public library, and the largest
livery stable in western Massachusetts. (The thirty-
eight horses were all saved.)

The water in the reservoir gave out. A steamer
was sent from Northampton to help but did not
arrive until daybreak. Emily was awakened by the
noise. Vinnie told her it was just the Fourth of July
celebration and took her to their mother's room.
Emily let Vinnie think she believed the story. She

didn't tell her that she knew the truth all along and was watching from her window.

In the summer of 1880 Emily had her last visit from Charles Wadsworth. No one knows what they discussed on that visit.

On November 8, 1880, Sarah Bernhardt, the celebrated French actress, made her American debut at Booth's Theater in New York City. Austin took his children to see her star with Edwin Booth in *Camille*. He often took them to New York galleries to expose them to the arts. Susan read French and Latin to them and taught them algebra and geometry.

Century of Dishonor by Helen Hunt Jackson was published in 1881. It was a sharply documented criticism of the U. S. government for its treatment of the Indians. In 1882, Helen was appointed a special commissioner to investigate conditions among the Indians of the California missions. While there, she consciously or unconsciously was getting the background and setting for her next novel. In October 1883, Helen told her husband she had dreamed an entire plot for a novel about the Indians of these missions.

In December, she went to New York and stayed at the Berkley Hotel while she wrote *Ramona*. It was published in 1884. The book was the most famous of her works and ranked with *Uncle Tom's Cabin* as one of the great moral novels of the century. Jackson was second only to Harriet Beecher Stowe in fame.

In 1881, Mabel Loomis Todd came to Amherst with her husband, David Peck Todd. She was twenty-five years old that summer. There was no way for anyone to know the effect she would have on all the Dickinsons and the major role she would play in their lives.

Mabel had an outgoing personality and all the social skills that Sue admired. She painted in oil and watercolor. She also played the piano seriously and well, which Emily appreciated. She never spoke with Emily, as Emily hid behind a door while Mabel played for her. But she did catch a glimpse once, through a doorway, of Emily flitting by in white. Mabel commented in her journal about Emily and her strange and remarkable poems. She considered Emily, in many respects, a genius.

Emily would sit on the stairs in the front hall and listen to Mabel play and sing. When Mabel was finished, Emily always sent a glass of wine to her on a silver salver, and with it either a piece of cake or a rose, and a poem, possibly written as she listened.

Mabel was well read and had ambitions as an author. She had several essays published while she was growing up. Her real-life heroine was Louisa May Alcott. When Mabel was nineteen, she had called on Louisa several times in Boston. Louisa was strongminded, independent, and literary—all the things Mabel admired.

Sophia Thoreau was a friend of Mabel's grandmother and was often with Louisa. Mabel's mother was Mary Alden Wilder, who had a direct lineage to Priscilla Alden of the *Mayflower*.

Mabel thought highly of Sue Dickinson when she first met her. Sue not only represented the social class that Mabel admired and wanted to join but was the leader of that class. Sue liked Mabel at

Mabel Loomis Todd

first, too. Mabel began giving piano lessons to Mattie.

Ned was twenty years old and a sophomore in college in March of 1882. He met and admired this new friend of his mother's. In fact, he became enchanted with Mabel, and they often went riding together. Finally, he fell in love with her, but that love was not returned.

Ned was not the only Dickinson male to admire Mabel's talents. Austin, who had never had much to do with Sue's social gatherings, found this new face to be much to his liking. He began escorting Mabel home, and they discovered mutual interests.

Charles Wadsworth died in April of that year, another of the important people in Emily's life. In May of 1882, Emily heard that Judge Lord was sick. She sent a telegram through Professor Chickering: "I asked the wires how you did, and attached my name." Emily was very upset that yet another of the people she loved was in danger of dying. She was relieved when news came that he was better.

By the fall of that year, trouble had flared up at the Dickinsons. Ned went to his mother and told her that Mabel was a flirt. He said that she had jilted him and was now after his father. Sue became extremely jealous. She had already begun to have doubts about Mabel being her friend. She had told Mabel a story about Emily and Vinnie that concerned their having rather loose morals. She warned Mabel to stay away from them. Mabel hadn't listened, or rather, she had decided to make up her own mind and had gone to call next door and become friends with Vinnie. Sue did not like to be crossed in any way, and this woman seemed to be going out of her way to do it.

Then Mrs. Dickinson died in November. Emily had devoted most of her time to her mother. It was difficult for everyone in the family, but worst for Emily. The house seemed strange to her with just herself and Vinnie left.

Sue continued to entertain in a lavish and expensive style. She would serve oyster stew at 10 P.M. for a break in the evening. Only those people Sue seemed to think were important were invited, and any that had disagreed with her over anything were banned from the events. Life became increasingly shallow at the Evergreens.

Austin stayed away from home more and more. He spent a lot of time at the mansion with his sisters. He wrote in his diary about "Sue and her crowd" and avoided them whenever possible.

Austin met Mabel behind the closed doors of the dining room at the mansion. Vinnie and Emily knew and were accessories to their meetings. Emily and Mabel were bound to each other by their mutual love of Austin. Austin spent so much time at the homestead that Emily wrote, "We almost forget that he ever passed to a wedded home."

On October 5, 1883, eight-year-old Gil died from typhoid fever. They had given him cool baths to try to break his fever, but it wasn't enough. The entire family grieved. Gil's last words in his delirium were, "Open the door, open the door, they are waiting for me." Emily said, "Anguish at last opened it and he ran to the little grave at his grandparents' feet. Who were waiting for him, all we possess we would give to know."

Gil and his playmates had tramped at will through the mansion, and Gil was at home there. The children accepted Emily as a friend with the powers to produce unexpected rewards. She talked to them as equals, and they considered it a treat to visit with her. She used to call to them from her bedroom window and lower baskets filled with cookies or small cakes.

Emily had been there the night Gil died. It was the first time in years that she had been at the Evergreens. Afterward, she went home and was ill in bed for weeks. Austin was equally upset. His depression seemed to rob him of his interest in life.

With Gil gone, there was not much home life left at the Evergreens. There seemed to be nothing to hold Austin and Sue together. Austin continued to see Mabel, and Sue couldn't do much about it. The social, civil, and religious tenets of the time prevented her from getting a divorce.

Every woman was a perpetual minor. If she married, she became the property of her husband. If she remained single, she was obliged to assign her property to a male guardian. No married woman was allowed to sue for breach of contract, to retain wages she earned for her work, or to receive damages for injury done to her person or character.

In every situation, the husband ruled. He was the arbiter of his wife's fate and fortune and the owner of her children. He could give or will away children without the mother's consent. Even if he proved to be a degenerate or drunkard, he became the children's sole custodian in the event of divorce.

Men were allowed to beat their wives, children, and dogs.

Women were not allowed to divorce their husbands even on grounds of physical cruelty. Austin was never cruel to Sue or his children. He went out of his way to avoid unpleasantness. Sue probably would not have divorced him even if she could have. She was too used to the life that she led and knew that as a divorceé she would be penniless or, even worse, a social outcast. That would have been the worst thing that could happen to Sue.

Emily and Helen Hunt Jackson continued to write to each other on a regular basis. Both were plagued by health problems. At times they lost touch, but overall, Helen was one of the few people that had a lifelong relationship with Emily.

In March 1884, Emily received word that Judge Lord had died. She collapsed when she heard the news. The doctor was called and said her condition was caused by nerves. He confined her to her bedroom indefinitely. Later that spring, she had her first attack of Bright's disease, a kidney disease that would eventually be fatal.

In June, Helen Hunt Jackson tripped on the stairs in her Colorado home. She was an invalid after that and also under a doctor's care. Emily and Helen wrote to each other of their illnesses throughout the winter. In the spring of 1885, Emily's disease grew worse, but then she seemed to get better for a while. Helen was not getting better, and she went to California on the advice of her physician.

Helen had a short story published in May 1885. She and Emily kept in touch for a while longer, then Emily read in the paper that Helen had died in San Francisco on August 12. Emily was shocked. She knew that Helen had been ill, but she had had no idea that her friend was dying.

Helen, however, had known. She wrote good-bye notes to her publishers that summer. She chose not to tell Emily, perhaps to keep from causing her more distress. Helen understood the creative mind and moods and possibly wanted to spare Emily the pain of losing another friend for as long as she could.

In November, Emily was ill again. The doctor forbade books or thought. That was fine for him to say, but he could not have known Emily. The books might have been kept from her, but her mind was never still.

In January 1886, a friend sent her a little book, *Called Back*, by Hugh Conway. She probably read it. Her illness continued to become worse, and she was confined to bed. The day before she died, she sent a note to her cousins Louisa and Fanny Norcross:

> *Little Cousins—*
> *called back,*
> *Emily*

Emily died on May 15, 1886, at the age of fifty-five. She had asked that when she died she be carried out the back door, around through her garden, through the opened barn doors from front to back, and finally through the grassy fields to the family plot. In this way she would always be in sight of her home.

Her wishes were granted. Before the coffin was closed, Vinnie put two heliotropes in by her hand to take to Judge Lord. Her white coffin was then carried by laborers, who had worked for her father, to her final resting place.

Chapter

⚜ELEVEN⚜

Vinnie, alone at the mansion, had to go through Emily's things. She found the packets of letters and poems that Emily had placed in her cherrywood bureau. They were marked to be burned unread when she died. Vinnie did burn the letters but could not bring herself to destroy the poetry. She knew that her sister had been writing but had no idea of the quantity of work she had produced.

Vinnie was practical and forthright in manner, and blunt in speech. She had helped Emily through emotional crises, remained quietly at home, maintained the house, and devoted herself to Emily. She had shared her confidences and protected her. It was her love of Emily that led to the eventual publication of her sister's poetry rather than its destruction.

Vinnie took the poems to Sue. Sue had no interest in them. She thought they would never sell because the public would not be interested in them. They were too different from what was expected.

Vinnie wanted to see Emily's poetry published, and she also needed the money. She did not have the income to live on the level that Austin and Sue did. She went to Mabel Loomis Todd with some of the poems and asked her for her help.

Mabel agreed with Vinnie about the quality of the work and thought that it ought to be published. Vinnie began taking poems to Mabel in secret night meetings. The clandestine arrangements were to avoid bringing the wrath of Sue down onto Vinnie.

Mabel and Austin continued to see each other whenever possible. Vinnie continued to offer the homestead as a meeting place. She was confidant, messenger, and scribe for them, often addressing envelopes to avoid the handwriting being identified. She welcomed Mabel as an ally against Sue.

David Todd also knew of the affair. He loved Mabel and revered Austin. He was a sweet and gentle man, and Mabel loved him as well as Austin. The entire town seemed to know, but no one would say anything. Most of them liked Austin and feared Sue. Sue was pretentious and encouraged Mattie and Ned to assume an attitude of superiority in the town and to their neighbors. This caused many families that were quite as good in background and attainments as the Dickinsons to dislike them.

Mabel began editing Emily's poems at the handsome quartered-oak desk that Austin gave her. She worked to convince Col. Higginson of the merit of the poems. He agreed to help edit and find a publisher. He also decided that they should all have titles. Emily had never given her poems titles.

Mabel changed some of the wording of the poems. She thought that some of them needed work.

In November of 1887, Mabel began to copy Emily's poems on a Hammond typewriter. By 1889, she had copied over two hundred of them, in addition to publishing an essay, "In September," and "The Sexton's Story," a romance. When the Hammond broke down, she continued copying on a less sophisticated, slower World typewriter.

Mabel and Col. Higginson edited and compiled three small volumes of Emily's poems. They were published in 1890, 1891, and 1892. At first, Mabel and Col. Higginson agreed to help the publisher with the cost of the printing. The publisher had doubts that the poems would sell. When they sold well, the entire cost was taken over by the publisher.

In 1894, they published a collection of Emily's letters. The letters Vinnie had burned were the ones Emily had received. A lot of letters she wrote to other people were saved and available.

Vinnie started becoming jealous of Mabel's success with Emily's poems, both as an editor and as a lecturer. She tried to have Mabel's name kept off the books. She knew that Sue would find out about it and know that Mabel had gotten the poems from Vinnie. She also felt that Emily's fame should reflect on her. She had devoted most of her life to Emily and felt she was entitled to any success stemming from Emily.

Mabel didn't care how any of them felt. She was doing a labor of love. She believed in the poetry, and she had Austin's backing. Nothing could stand in the way of her goal.

Then Austin died on August 16, 1895. Ned, in a gesture of kindness, arranged for Mabel to be in the house while the family was at lunch. Mabel was able to have a few moments this last time with

Austin to say goodbye. All the shops in Amherst closed in honor of Austin on the day of his funeral.

Austin left the homestead and his share of his father's estate to Vinnie, two pictures to Mabel, and the rest to Sue. He and Vinnie had also owned a strip of land adjoining the Todds that they had been left by their father. Vinnie signed a deed of gift at Austin's request so that the Todds could have it. Austin did not put this in his will, as he trusted Vinnie.

In 1898, at Sue's urging, Vinnie filed suit for the land. She knew she was being disloyal to the Todds and to Austin. She lied about the gift of deed. Sue didn't want or need the land to come back into the family. All she was interested in was the public humiliation of Mabel.

It was a nasty court case. Unsavory gossip was brought out about Mabel and Austin and the whole town fed on it and took sides. It was difficult to understand why Vinnie would do such a thing to Mabel and to David Todd. David had gone every Saturday night to wind Vinnie's clocks, and one time accompanied her to Norwich, Connecticut, for the funeral of a relative. The Todds had never been anything but kind to Vinnie. The lawsuit was a cover for a personal feud between Sue and Mabel. The Todds decided finally that it was not worth having their private lives aired in public, so they just moved and everything was dropped.

Over five hundred poems had been published by this time. Mabel stopped editing and packed over 665 poems away in a camphorwood chest.

This might have been where the story of Emily and her poetry ended. In 1870, Emerson had expressed a wish that Julia Ward Howe had been a native of Massachusetts because "We have no such poetess in New England." He had no way of knowing that at that time Emily Dickinson's bureau contained most of her best work. The world might never have known. As late as 1922, Robert Hillyer wrote in *The Freeman*, "It is doubtful if Emily Dickinson will ever be famous."

Ned died in May 1898, the last male member of the family. He had never shown any interest in the poems. Vinnie died on August 31, 1899. She did not live to see fame and honor bestowed on Emily.

After Sue died in May 1913, her daughter, Martha Dickinson Bianchi, gathered the poems that her Aunt Vinnie still had in the mansion, and those that Emily had written to her mother that were saved. She published them piecemeal in 1914 and 1937.

Mabel Todd died in 1945, and the camphorwood chest went to her daughter, Millicent Todd Bingham. Millicent published over 600 poems that her mother had edited and copied but not published. She also published a collection of letters to and from Emily and Col. Higginson that had been in her mother's possession.

Volumes came from both sides of the feuding families. The ongoing hard feelings handicapped all biographers who wanted to learn about Emily. Letters were edited before publication, some by the people they were sent to. All the books claimed to be the authority on the subject of Emily. The interviews that were conducted were with people who tried to remember what had happened fifty years prior to the questions.

It is claimed that the dates on some of the

poems may have been changed by Martha Bianchi to show that Emily and Sue were friends to the end. Others claim that this is not true. It is difficult to believe that Emily would continue a close relationship with anyone who had hurt her brother, especially someone who seemed to have the "empty thoughts" and "plated wares" that Emily despised so much.

There are many contradictions concerning the Myth of Amherst, as Emily was called. No one knows the whole truth. Those that knew are all gone. We may never know much about her personal life.

What we do know is that she left us a legacy in the 1,775 poems and 1,049 letters that are known. The subject of some of her poems is not clear. Interpretation of her work can only be guesswork. What she meant and what she felt when writing was something only she knew.

Perhaps it is better that we don't know. We can let each of her poems speak to us as individuals.

Some of them, or maybe all of them, might only be expressions of the poet working at her craft and enjoying herself. Emily loved words. She loved to play with them like a child plays with a set of building blocks. She liked the way they looked on the paper, the way they felt as she wrote them, and the way they sounded within her mind. By changing them she could build new and wonderful things.

The love poems may have been about a real lover. But no one really knows if such a person existed, and as widely read as Emily was, she could have learned all about love from her readings. She did not seem to have one single totally satisfying relationship, even in her family. They accepted her, but did not seem to really understand her. Everything was on her terms. Anyone who could not accept those terms was not in her life.

We can best understand Emily Dickinson through her poetry. For example, we know that she loved her books and often wrote about the joys of reading:

> He ate and drank the precious words,
> His spirit grew robust;
> He knew no more that he was poor,
> Nor that his frame was dust.
> He danced along the dingy days,
> And this bequest of wings
> Was but a book. What liberty
> A loosened spirit brings![1]

As much as she enjoyed the words of others, she did not think it desirable to be famous:

> I'm nobody! Who are you?
> Are you nobody, too?
> Then there's a pair of us—don't tell!
> They'd banish us, you know.
>
> How dreary to be somebody!
> How public, like a frog
> To tell your name the livelong day
> To an admiring bog!

She wrote about love and marriage as if that is what she wanted most:

[1] All quoted poems are from *The Poems of Emily Dickinson*, ed. by Martha Dickinson Bianchi and Alfred Leete Hampson, (Boston: Little, Brown and Company, 1944).

Forever at his side to walk
The smaller of the two,
Brain of his brain, blood of his blood,
Two lives, one Being, now.

Forever of his fate to taste.
If grief, the largest part—
If joy, to put my piece away
For that beloved heart.

All life to know each other—
Whom we can never learn,
And by and by a change called 'Heaven'—
Rapt neighborhood of men,
Just finding out what puzzled us
Without the lexicon!

She wrote about lost love. Poems such as these
added to the rumors she had a secret lover:

You left me, sweet, two legacies,—
A legacy of love
A Heavenly Father would content,
Had He the offer of;

You left me boundaries of pain
Capacious as the sea,
Between eternity and time,
Your consciousness and me.

She looked for peace within herself. Perhaps at
times she hoped that whatever force was driving
her would ease and she could lead a normal life:

I many times thought peace had come,
When peace was far away;
As wrecked men deem they sight the land
At centre of the sea,

And struggle slacker, but to prove,
As hopelessly as I,
How many fictious shores
Before the harbor lie.

She had no regrets about not belonging to a formal
church:

Some keep the Sabbath going to church;
I keep it staying at home,
With a bobolink for a chorister,
And an orchard for a dome.

Some keep the Sabbath in surplice;
I just wear my wings,
And instead of tolling the bell for church,
Our little sexton sings.

God preaches,—a noted clergyman,—
And the sermon is never long;
So, instead of getting to heaven at last,
I'm going all along!

Letters from friends were important to her. They
were her link to the outside world. She savored
every word of them, and read them where she
could concentrate:

The way I read a letter's this:
'Tis first I lock the door,
And push it with my fingers next,
For transport it be sure.

And then I go the furthest off
To counteract a knock;
Then draw my little letter forth
And softly pick its lock.

Then, glancing narrow at the wall,
And narrow at the floor,
For firm conviction of a mouse
Not exorcised before,

Peruse how infinite I am
To—no one that you know!
And sigh for lack of heave,—but not
The heaven the creeds bestow.

When she wrote about death, at times it seems that she was almost writing about her own, the way it would be:

She went as quiet as the dew
From a familiar flower.
Not like the dew did she return
At the accustomed hour!

She dropt as softly as a star
From out my summer's eve;
Less skillful than Leverrier
Its sorer to believe!

Emily demanded a lot from the people in her life, perhaps too much. She did not seem to have, or accept, casual friends. She was too intense for most people and didn't understand their concerns for everyday things. She took the ordinary and made it extraordinary. She liked distance in a physical sense.

That seems to be why most of her friendships were through letters only. She could weigh each word before she wrote it, or change it after it was written. She couldn't do that in a verbal conversation.

She once wrote to a friend, "How lovely are the wiles of words." Maybe some of the things she wrote were used only to beguile those who read. She made people think.

She was as much a mystery then as she is now. In one letter to Col. Higginson, she wrote, "All men say 'What' to me, but I thought it a fashion." The way she spoke must have been as unique as the way she wrote.

We do know that while she lived Emily was constantly looking for some evidence of an afterlife. In a way, she found it in her poetry, which lives on. She was close to God even though she had no assurance of Him. She kept her faith all her life. She clung to nature as her teacher and her quiet routine at home. Through her writing, perhaps, we can be a little closer to her.

This World is not Conclusion.
A Species stands beyond—
Invisable, as Music—
But positive, as Sound.

Recommended Reading

Anderson, Charles R. *Emily Dickinson's Poetry: Stairway of Surprise.* New York: Holt, Rinehart and Winston, 1960.
Benet, Laura. *The Mystery of Emily Dickinson.* New York: Dodd, Mead, 1974.
Bianchi, Martha Dickinson. *Emily Dickinson Face to Face.* Hamden, CT: Archon, 1970.
Bianchi, Martha Dickinson, and Alfred Leete Hampson. *The Poems of Emily Dickinson.* Boston: Little, Brown, 1944.
Bingham, Millicent Todd. *Emily Dickinson's Home.* New York: Dover, 1967.
Cleveland, Rose E. *The Social Mirror.* St Louis, Mo.: J.L. Herbert Publishing Company, 1888.
Fisher, Aileen, and Olive Rabe. *We Dickinsons.* New York: Atheneum, 1966.
Jenkins, MacGregor. *Emily Dickinson, Friend and Neighbor.* Boston: Little, Brown, 1930.
Johnson, Thomas H. *Emily Dickinson, An Interpretive Biography.* Cambridge: Harvard University Press, Belknap Press, 1955.
Johnson, Thomas H., ed. *The Poems of Emily Dickinson.* 3 vols. Cambridge: Harvard University Press, Belknap Press, 1955.
Johnson, Thomas H., and Theodora Ward, eds. *The Letters of Emily Dickinson.* Cambridge: Harvard University Press, Belknap Press, 1958.
Leyda, Jay. *The Years and Hours of Emily Dickinson.* New Haven, Conn.: Yale University Press, 1960.

Longsworth, Polly. *Austin and Mabel*. New York: Farrar, Straus & Giroux, 1984.
Longsworth, Polly. *Emily Dickinson: Her Letters to the World*. New York: Thomas Y. Crowell, 1965.
Mudge, Jean McClure. *Emily Dickinson & the Image of Home*. Amherst, Mass.: The University of Amherst Press, 1975.
Pollit, Josephine. *Emily Dickinson, The Human Background of Her Poetry*. New York: Cooper Square Publishers, 1970.
Sangster, Margaret E. *The Art of Home-making*. New York: The Christian Herald Bible House, 1898.
Sewall, Richard Benson. *The Life of Emily Dickinson, Vol. 1 and Vol. 2*. New York: Farrar, Straus & Giroux, 1975.
Wells, Henry W. *Introduction to Emily Dickinson*. New York: Pochard & Co. 1947; Reprint: Hendricks House, Inc., 1959.
Wells, Anna Mary. *Dear Preceptor: The Life and Times of Thomas Wentworth Higginson*. Boston: Houghton Mifflin, 1963.
Whicher, George Frisbie. *This Was a Poet: A Critical Biography of Emily Dickinson*. New York: Charles Scribner's Sons, 1938.

Index

j   THAYER, BONITA E.
B
DIC   Emily Dickinson